Words from the Wise

Exploring Biblical Wisdom

Paul Luckraft

malcolm down
PUBLISHING

Copyright © Paul Luckraft 2024
First published 2024 by Malcolm Down Publishing Ltd
www.malcolmdown.co.uk

28 27 26 25 24   7 6 5 4 3 2 1

The right of Paul Luckraft to be identified as the author of this work has been asserted by him in accordance with the Copyright, Designs and Patents Act 1988.

All rights reserved. No part of this publication may be reproduced, stored in a retrieval system, or transmitted in any other form or by any means, electronic, mechanical, photocopying, recording or otherwise, without the prior permission of the publisher.

British Library Cataloguing in Publication Data
A catalogue record for this book is available from the British Library.

ISBN 978-1-915046-98-7

Unless otherwise indicated, Scripture quotations taken from the Holy Bible, New International Version (Anglicised edition) Copyright ©1979, 1984, 2011 by Biblica.
Used by permission of Hodder & Stoughton Publishers,
an Hachette UK company.
All rights reserved.
'NIV' is a registered trademark of Biblica.
UK trademark number 1448790.

Scripture quotations marked 'NKJV' are taken from the Holy Bible, New King James Version®.
Copyright © 1982 by Thomas Nelson. Used by permission.
All rights reserved.

Cover design by Esther Kotecha
Art direction by Sarah Grace

Printed in the UK

In today's church, there exists a clamour of interest in the more glamorous spiritual gifts, such as prophecy, healing and miracles. But surely there is much more need to gain the biblical gift of wisdom.

This illuminating book offers a much-needed study on this neglected topic. While focusing on the traditional wisdom books of Proverbs, Job and Ecclesiastes, Paul Luckraft gleans much from the overall teaching of the Bible, with separate chapters, for example, on the wisdom contained in the Psalms and the New Testament epistle of James.

The book is an in-depth, comprehensive study, written with the ordinary Christian in mind, but containing much that Bible teachers, preachers and students of the Word of God might also learn. There are even chapters on: 'Preaching from the Book of Proverbs'; 'Proverbs 22:6, A Case Study'; 'Wisdom in the Apocrypha'; and a section on Christ, our supreme example, whom the apostle Paul calls 'The Wisdom of God'.

Ultimately, the author tells us, 'Wisdom is about how to live life well and handle situations properly . . . Wisdom is essentially practical.'

It's time that believers everywhere began to 'wise up' and seek after the Lord, 'who gives generously to all without finding fault' (James 1:5). Many of us might also benefit from leaning on the rich wisdom contained within this book.

Tom Lennie
Executive Editor, *Prophecy Today*
Author of *Scotland: Land of Many Revivals* and *Island Aflame: The Famed Lewis Awakening that Never Occurred and the Glorious Revival that Did*

Looking at the state of the world today it could be said there is a need for wisdom above all else. The same might also apply to our own individual lives. It is surprising, then, that the wisdom books of the Bible are probably the least-read portions. Often Christians struggle to make sense of Proverbs, Job and Ecclesiastes in the Old Testament, nor do they focus in the New on Christ being 'the wisdom of God'.

This new book from Paul Luckraft is an excellent introduction to the biblical wisdom literature. Whilst there are succinct summaries of the content, the real gain is in learning how to read these texts. Paul has some wonderful nuggets of information that help clarify our understanding and bring the books to life. The handling of Ecclesiastes in particular is outstanding. All the issues are carefully considered, though some may still be challenged by his conclusion that we should 'abandon any assertion that Solomon wrote' it.

The Old Testament wisdom material should lead us to seeing the importance of Christ as the source of wisdom. In this book there is a real integration of both Testaments, with a good analysis of James, a letter often played down.

Paul writes that where wisdom comes from and how we get it are crucial questions. This book will show you the answers.

Revd Ian Farley
Rector, St John's Buckhurst Hill

I've been teaching the Bible for fifty years and have usually avoided Proverbs, Ecclesiastes and Job. Paul has done a great job in helping me make sense of these difficult books. He has distilled the essence of the wisdom found in these books and made it accessible to all. Above all, this very readable book has given me fresh enthusiasm for the biblical wisdom literature.

I would say, 'If anyone lacks wisdom, let him ask God' – but also get this book!

David Serle
Bible teacher and contributor to *Sword* Magazine

Words from the Wise is a gem of a book. As well as providing a rich exploration of the Bible's wisdom literature, Paul gives us the gift of how to read these passages. Jesus once described what a teacher in his kingdom would do as '[bringing] out of his storeroom new treasures as well as old' (Matthew 13:52). This is exactly what Paul has done in opening up the ancient wisdom of scripture and bringing fresh insights to help us to apply it to our lives today.

Revd Canon John McGinley
Leader of the Myriad Church Planting Programme
Author of *The Church of Tomorrow*

Paul's teaching is always informative, bringing clarity to difficult parts of the Bible. In our series on the book of James, his message on wisdom was particularly helpful.

Mari McLoughlin
Church leader

'Pay attention and turn your ear
to the sayings of the wise.'

Proverbs 22:17

'Where can wisdom be found?'

Job 28:12

'If any of you lacks wisdom,
you should ask God.'

James 1:5

Acknowledgements

The material for *Words from the Wise* started life as a series of short talks for my website. These 'coffee-cup' talks of around fifteen minutes were tweaked slightly to form the chapters of the book you are now holding. This approach had worked well for me before when writing my first two books, and feedback from those on the receiving end had suggested it worked well for them too. I hope this continues to remain the case with my latest book.

I am extremely grateful to all at my own church who gave me regular encouragement and support during the making of the original talks. Thanks also to those who provided opportunities for me to test this material by teaching it in various gatherings, online and in person. Plus a special thanks to those who took the time and trouble to read the initial draft of the manuscript and provide endorsements.

I am especially indebted to Frances, not only for her efficient management of my website, but also for her sterling work in helping with the preparation of the manuscript and for taking on the laborious task of compiling the index.

As always, I am grateful to those at Malcolm Down Publishing who guided me through the whole process of producing this book. Special thanks go to my editor, Louise, for her usual prompt and efficient work, and to Malcolm Down for his clear advice and expertise. Thanks also to the graphic designers for the front cover.

Finally, I wish to acknowledge that in compiling the original talks I greatly benefited from reading the following books:

Bill Cotton, *Job* (Christian Focus Publications)

James L. Crenshaw, *Old Testament Wisdom* (John Knox Press)

Graeme Goldsworthy, *Gospel and Wisdom* (Paternoster Press)

Derek Kidner, *The Message of Ecclesiastes* (IVP)

Derek Kidner, *The Wisdom of Proverbs, Job and Ecclesiastes* (IVP)

Eric Lane, *Proverbs* (Christian Focus Publications)

Dan Phillips, *God's Wisdom in Proverbs* (Kress Biblical Resources)

R.B.Y. Scott, *The Way of Wisdom* (The Macmillan Company)

R.C. Sproul, *What Is Biblical Wisdom?* (Ligonier Ministries)

For those who want to listen to the original talks, over a cup of coffee or otherwise, these can be found on my website www.orchardseeds.com.

Contents

Introduction	15
1. Defining Wisdom	21
2. The Fear of the Lord	29
3. Listen, My Son	37
4. Meet Lady Wisdom	45
5. A Tale of Two Houses	53
6. Proverbs: The Collections	61
7. Proverbs: Their Nature and Style	69
8. Proverbs 22:6, A Case Study	79
9. Proverbs: Thirty Sayings of the Wise	89
10. Proverbs: Chapters 25 to 29	99
11. Proverbs: Chapter 30, The Sayings of Agur	105
12. Proverbs: Chapter 31, Sayings of King Lemuel and a Poem on the Wife of Noble Character	113
13. Preaching from the Book of Proverbs	121
14. Job: An Introduction	125
15. Job: Meet the Cast	133
16. Job: Going Round in Cycles	141

17.	Job: Chapter 28, A Wisdom Poem	149
18.	Job: Chapters 38 to 42, And God Said . . .	157
19.	Job: Summary and Conclusions	167
20.	Ecclesiastes: Meet Your Teacher	175
21.	Ecclesiastes: Words of the Teacher	185
22.	Ecclesiastes: More Words of the Teacher	193
23.	Ecclesiastes: Some Final Thoughts	203
24.	The Relationship Between Proverbs, Job and Ecclesiastes	211
25.	Wisdom in the Psalms	219
26.	Wisdom in the Apocrypha	227
27.	Learning from Solomon	237
28.	Christ, The Wisdom of God	247
29.	James and the Gift of Wisdom	255
30.	Two Kinds of Wisdom	263
31.	The Nature and Value of Wisdom	269
32.	In Conclusion	275
33.	Index of Scripture	279

Introduction

The Bible has much to say about wisdom, both in the Old Testament and the New. Indeed, some parts of the Bible are devoted entirely to this theme and so are referred to as wisdom literature, suggesting this is not just their primary purpose but their sole intention. We will engage with these books in some detail as we can only understand the biblical wisdom tradition by immersing ourselves in its literature. Their distinctive literary forms and characteristic interests, plus the vocabulary and phrases they use, are vital in enabling us to draw out the main themes of biblical wisdom.

So what are these books? Three stand out in particular: Proverbs, Ecclesiastes and Job. These are most commonly regarded as the wisdom books of the Old Testament, but for many Christians, these are not usually the most frequently trodden paths within the Hebrew Scriptures. Proverbs is perhaps the best known of these but is often seen as little more than a list of one-liners, single sentences forming a torrent of metaphors and similes lacking any kind of narrative and with no obvious pattern. Dipping in and out seems to be the best way to approach this book rather than settling down to a satisfying session of continual reading.

By contrast, Job is a continuous narrative but is usually shunned as being too long and, let's be honest, rather boring in places. Some portions might be well known but as a whole it is hardly anyone's favourite. The temptation is usually to scan it quickly, sum up its message and move on to something more enjoyable.

Whether that 'something' is Ecclesiastes is rather debatable. Although shorter, Ecclesiastes is seen as being extremely pessimistic in outlook and rather confusing to come to terms with. How does it relate to faith? Indeed why is it in the Bible at all? These are questions we will need to dig into.

Equally important for our consideration is the relationship that these three books have with each other and how individually they contribute towards the concept of wisdom as a whole. Are they complementary or contradictory? Do they represent different aspects of the same wisdom tradition or do they clash with each other and offer totally contrary and irreconcilable viewpoints?

In our studies of these three books, we will not be able to provide the same depth that individual commentaries can bring, but nor will we shy away from the issues and challenges they throw up and which have occupied scholarly debate over time.

Overall, our aim is twofold. Firstly, to encourage Christians not to neglect these books. It may not initially be easy to see how they can be part of devotional Bible reading, yet these books all relate to human experience. We need them as they challenge us to reflect and respond in some way. We hope to inspire Christians to give these books a second chance.

Secondly, for those who are Bible teachers, preachers, or students of the Word of God, there should be enough in this book to inform and enlighten them. It is hoped this will enhance their own studies and provide material for further lessons and messages.

Some people may want to count the Song of Songs and the book of Daniel among the wisdom literature, the former as it is associated with Solomon and the latter as parts of the book are seen as prophetic wisdom related through dreams. However, we will not be including these. We have enough to come to terms with as it is! And it can be argued they are rather on the periphery of biblical wisdom rather than central to its main points. However, some psalms are categorised as wisdom psalms and so we will consider what they contribute to our theme.

Then there are other Jewish wisdom books that weren't included in the biblical canon. Two of these are worth mentioning in our studies. These are the Wisdom of Solomon and the Wisdom of Jesus Ben Sirach or sometimes just Sirach for short. You may have heard of the latter under the title of Ecclesiasticus (not to be confused with Ecclesiastes which *is* in the Bible! Nor, of course, is this Jesus the same as the son of Joseph and Mary!). These two books are part of the Apocrypha, so they are not regarded as having the same level of inspiration or authority as the biblical books but are still worth reading. Knowing something about them does add to the whole wisdom picture, so we will briefly consider them also.

Overall there will be many intriguing facets for us to explore along the way. One is why the Old Testament contains wisdom material from outside the nation of Israel.

Can this really represent God's word to us? Another aspect for our consideration is how wisdom was taught in ancient Israel and what it meant to be counted as wise. The term 'wisdom' refers to more than just a style or genre of book. It represents a specific understanding of reality, offering guidance on how the world works and how to live within it. Are there any lessons for us here? Indeed, is biblical wisdom still relevant today at all?

Another fascinating feature is how wisdom was often personified (that is, treated as though it was a person). This literary device is frequently seen within the wisdom literature and is regarded as helpful in explaining the nature and characteristics of wisdom.

Of course, no study of biblical wisdom can ignore the figure most associated with wisdom in the Old Testament, namely Solomon. But just how wise was he? What can we learn from his wisdom?

In all this, we will need to define wisdom carefully, making sure this definition is not too wide or too narrow as to be unhelpful. Studying the Hebrew and Greek words used, as well as the various contexts in which wisdom is mentioned, will be important in this respect. It will also be useful to consider the opposite of wisdom, what the Bible calls 'folly'. What exactly does this mean and how do we avoid it?

As always with a whole Bible approach to a topic we must take into account the progressive revelation of scripture, and in particular the issue of connections and contrasts between the two Testaments. In the case of biblical wisdom, we must value Paul's great statement that Christ is 'the wisdom of God' (1 Cor. 1:24). Here is the centrepiece of what the New Testament has to say on this topic. It is also the ultimate expression of biblical wisdom towards which our whole study is heading. Alongside this, there is the role of wisdom within the spiritual gifts which the risen Christ has given to his church to enable us to live according to his will and purpose.

So, all in all, the amount of material on this important biblical theme, and the complexity of some of it, can be overwhelming. Organising it in a coherent way is difficult. There is bound to be some overlap and recapitulation as we work our way steadily through the scriptures.

Although it is sensible to start with the Old Testament wisdom books, we must mention at this point the one book in the New Testament which is also said to come into the category of wisdom literature, a rather isolated case, you may say. This is the book of James, usually regarded as a letter, or more specifically a circular letter, as it was not sent to a particular individual or place but intended generally for Jewish believers in Jesus who were scattered among the Gentile nations, rather than living in or near Jerusalem where James was the leader of the Christian community.

Within this letter there are several important statements about wisdom. For instance in James 3:15-17 we read about two kinds of wisdom, categorised as 'heavenly' and 'earthly', according to their origins. These need to be clearly distinguished and we will discuss them later.

But there is one statement earlier in James which has always struck me as significant and which sparked off my whole investigation. It acted as the catalyst that launched my long journey across the whole span of scripture. Above all, it created a desire to understand better the challenges and benefits that would arise if we were to 'pay attention ... to the sayings of the wise' (see Prov. 22:17).

The statement which made such an impact on me is in James 1:5. It reads, 'If any of you lacks wisdom, you should ask God, who gives generously to all without finding fault, and it will be given to you.'

How intriguing! But can this really be true? Free wisdom! What an offer! Who would want to turn that down? But suspicions can easily set in. Is this genuine? If something sounds too good to be true we usually suspect a catch somewhere. As we undertake our lengthy exploration into biblical wisdom, let's keep this verse constantly in mind. What a prospect ahead of us. As we persevere through our studies, which might at times seem demanding and difficult, here is the promise that will keep us going.

Meanwhile, our journey begins with what most people would usually think of first when asked to name an Old Testament wisdom book, namely Proverbs. But to start off on the right footing we must investigate the Hebrew word for wisdom found in that book and elsewhere in the Old Testament. So our first chapter is dedicated to a single word: *hokmah*.

Chapter One

Defining Wisdom

We said in the introduction that of all the books in the biblical wisdom literature, Proverbs is the best place to begin as it is the book most people are more familiar with. It is also the most appropriate in other ways. It contains many of the threads that we need to draw out of the wisdom literature in general and it also sets up a better appreciation of the other books to come, both in terms of comparison and contrast. But before all this we should examine the particular Hebrew words for 'wisdom' and 'wise', and see what they mean within the context of particular verses.

Hebrew words are built upon a root system of (usually) three consonants. In the case of wisdom these consonants are h-k-m where the initial h is pronounced 'ch' as at the end of 'loch'. From this root we get *hokmah*, which is the noun 'wisdom', and *hakam*, which is the adjective 'wise'. It is worth noting that *hokmah* is a feminine word, which may partly explain why, when wisdom is personified, it is as a female (see Prov. chapter 9 for example).

Another point about the word *hokmah* is that it has no plural form, so we cannot talk about 'wisdoms' as though there were more than one. However, as we shall see, we can think of different strands or applications of wisdom under the one main meaning.

For those more statistically minded, it is estimated that the Hebrew root h-k-m occurs around 318 times in the Old Testament, with well over half of these in Proverbs, Job and Ecclesiastes, which probably accounts for them being designated as wisdom literature. The noun *hokmah* occurs slightly more often than the adjective *hakam*, though we should add that *hakam* also appears a few times in a verbal form when you might find it translated as 'to act wisely, to make someone wise or to show oneself to be wise'.

With such a multitude of appearances throughout the Old Testament we might expect that both of these words feature in a wide range of situations, and this is indeed the case. There is a rich variety to the meaning and usage of both 'wisdom' and 'wise'. We cannot survey all the possible instances but we do need a certain number to get the full picture.

The first occurrence of *hakam* is found in Genesis 41:8, where the wise men of Pharaoh's court are summoned to help him over some bad dreams from the previous night which were still troubling him. We are not told what kind of wisdom they were supposed to possess but clearly it did not extend to interpreting Pharaoh's nightmares. Joseph, on the other hand, had that kind of wisdom or discernment which he not only recognised as a gift from God but also as means of enhancing his position with Pharaoh (see Gen. 41:16, 33, 39).

We meet Pharaoh's wise men again in Exodus 7:11 when they are summoned to reproduce the same miracles that were performed by Moses and Aaron. It seems that in pagan cultures generally there were groups of wise men or counsellors who practised magic and divination, including the interpretation of dreams. For instance, we read about the wise men of Babylon (Jer. 50:35), of Tyre (Ezek. 27:8-9) and of Edom (Obad. v8). Those in Babylon feature in the story of Daniel where, in Daniel chapter 2, there is again the matter of a troubling dream. This time it was Nebuchadnezzar who suffered a disturbed night. He demanded that his wise men tell him not only what the dream meant but what was actually in it. This, of course, they could not do, but Daniel turned to God for the wisdom he needed. In Daniel 2:20 he praises God that wisdom belongs to him alone, then in verse 21 asserts that God gives that wisdom to the wise, and then in verse 23 he thanks God for giving this wisdom to him, before telling Nebuchadnezzar everything he wants to know, at the same time making it clear that no wise man could have done this, only God in heaven (v27).

In these stories about Joseph and Daniel and the interpretation of dreams, we get our first glimpse that there are two kinds of wisdom, earthly and heavenly, as James mentions in his letter (Jas 3:13-18) and which we will come back to time and again. What we learn here in the Old Testament is that the source of true wisdom lies with God alone. He will provide it for us if we ask in faith. All human attempts to produce our own wisdom separate from God will fail.

Most people know that at the time of the birth of Jesus wise men (or magi) came from the east seeking the one born king of the Jews (Matt. 2:1-2). There has been much debate as to who they were or, to use our terms above, whether their wisdom was heavenly or earthly. It is noticeable that they knew something in advance about the birth of a messiah and that they twice received God's guidance: a star to get them to Jerusalem and a dream to send them home via a different route to avoid another encounter with King Herod. It may be that 'came from the east' refers to Babylon and that they were descended from Jews who had not returned from exile there. Perhaps they were of the same tradition as the wise men that Daniel had been part of, in which case their wisdom was true wisdom, but we will leave further speculation on this for others to follow up.

Returning to the Old Testament we find another aspect of true God-given wisdom, this time based upon practical skills and abilities. This first occurs in Exodus 28:3, where God says, 'Tell all the skilled workers to whom I have given wisdom in such matters that they are to make garments for Aaron, for his consecration, so that he may serve me as priest.'

Another classic example is that of Bezalel who, together with many skilled co-workers, was chosen by God to make all kinds of objects for the tabernacle. Regarding Bezalel, God declared, 'I have filled him with the Spirit of God, with wisdom, with understanding, with knowledge and with all kinds of skills . . .' (Exod. 31:2-11, see also Exod. 35:30ff). The various skills of Bezalel and his associates included working in precious metals and wood, as well as weaving, embroidery and many kinds of artistic crafts. The Hebrew words for 'skilled' and 'skilful' are related to that for wisdom, and these technical skills or special abilities are seen as being endowed by God, so they are also part of true wisdom. A later example of this involves preparations for the Temple, where David declares that there are craftsmen beyond number who are skilled in every kind of work (1 Chr. 22:15-16).

In similar vein there is also the curious case of those who make idols being called wise in what they do. We see this in Jeremiah 10:9 and also in Isaiah 40:20 where their particular skill is shown in making an idol that won't topple over! This is still true *hokmah* even if misapplied. The wisdom is found in the skill used rather than the object produced.

Overall, we find that the Hebrew concept of wisdom is not restricted to intellectual powers. It has a much wider range of meaning which includes practical abilities and skills. Basically it is knowing what is needed to accomplish a particular task within various spheres of activity. So although the principle translation of *hakam* remains as 'wise', there are several alternatives such as skilled or skilful or being a craftsman of some kind. Likewise, *hokmah* is still mainly 'wisdom' but it can also be skill or ability or, in one interesting verse, wits.

That verse is Psalm 107:27, where we read that sailors caught up in a fierce storm were 'at their wits' end'. Literally, their wisdom was swallowed up or overwhelmed by the situation. They were confused and had lost their ability to cope with what they faced. Their usual wisdom failed them in such extreme circumstances.

Another fascinating example involves animals. In Proverbs 30:24-28 four particular creatures are described as being 'extremely wise'. These creatures may be small or powerless, like the ant or hyrax (similar to a small rabbit or an oversized guinea pig) but they display high levels of cunning and ingenuity. They show their wisdom by knowing how to store up food for the winter months and how to make a home for themselves in difficult circumstances. In short, they know how to survive. And that can take a lot of wisdom at times!

We now have enough of a picture of the nature of wisdom in the Old Testament to be able to summarise what we have found. The words *hakam* and *hokmah* are important elements of the Old Testament generally but are not so much about religious ritual or creedal faith as gaining a mastery of living in accordance with God's ways.

Wisdom is not primarily intellectual or academic, nor is it purely an abstract concept. It often refers to skilled labour of some kind, or technical expertise and capability. It is never merely a matter of knowing facts, but of recognising how to apply them successfully to whatever is the task at hand. Wisdom is essentially practical.

But being wise is not just about human achievements. There is a divine aspect to wisdom. It should impact our moral and spiritual lives. Just as a craftsman is skilled in his trade, the wise man has become accomplished in living a life that is pleasing to God. He has learnt to receive true wisdom as a gift from God, and with this steer his way through life's many storms. He can thus cope better with the vagaries of life and find personal order and well-being in all things.

The wise man has gained an enhanced sense of making the right choice at the right time. Consistency in doing this is an indication of maturity and progress along the road of wisdom. In short, wisdom helps us to survive and thrive. The wise man is someone who has mastered something, and ultimately that something is life itself and, in particular, life with God.

In the next chapter we move on to consider something that the wisdom literature in general, and Proverbs in particular, mentions regularly, namely 'the fear of the Lord'. But what exactly is this fear?

Chapter Two

The Fear of the Lord

In our exploration of the topic of biblical wisdom we will be starting with the book of Proverbs, where we repeatedly meet the expression 'The fear of the LORD'. This is not a popular concept today. Have you ever heard a sermon or teaching on this? But we do need to understand what this means especially as we read that 'the fear of the LORD is the beginning of wisdom' (Prov. 9:10; see also Ps. 111:10).

A similar statement is found in Job 28:28. 'The fear of the Lord – that is wisdom.' In addition, the opening section of the book of Proverbs comes to a climax with, 'The fear of the LORD is the beginning of knowledge' (Prov. 1:7). Likewise in Proverbs 2:5 we read: 'You will understand the fear of the LORD and find the knowledge of God.' Moreover, many other verses in Proverbs mention the fear of the Lord in one context or another (see Prov. 1:29, 3:7, 8:13, 10:27, 14:26-27, 15:16, 15:33, 16:6, 19:23, 22:4, 23:17). Why is this phrase found so often in the wisdom literature?

The wisdom of ancient Israel had much in common with that of other cultures at the time but it also had its own distinctive features and a need to relate their pursuit of wisdom to their own God. So it is no surprise to find a phrase like 'the fear of the Lord' among their wisdom writings. But why 'fear'? What does this signify?

The Hebrew word for fear is formed from a different root from that of, say, dread or fright. So the phrase *yirat Adonai* does not denote a cringing terror or being scared of God. In common parlance we talk about putting the fear of God into someone, but that is not what is meant here. Rather this is reverential awe, a form of devotion based upon the holiness of an Almighty God, an awareness of the presence of the Supreme Being. Words other than fear could be used, such as awe, reverence or respect, but watering down the phraseology may not capture the true essence of what this is about. It would be better to add an adjective, such as *holy* fear, to get the main idea across.

No analogy is perfect but this illustration might help. Those who live on the coast have a special relationship with the sea. They enjoy the sounds and smells, the sight of something vast and immeasurable, stretching to the distant horizon and beyond. They may also find pleasure in pursuits such as paddling, swimming, surfing and sailing. But those who live on the coast also know the dangers of the sea. Currents can sweep you away, tides can cut you off, boats can sink, which is why we have lifeguards, lifeboats and lighthouses. Enjoy the sea but respect its power. When it comes to the fear of the Lord, be aware of who he is and who we are; what he is like and what we are like; he is the Creator, we are the creature; he is holy, we are not.

It is important to realise there is no contradiction between 'the fear of the Lord' and biblical commands to 'fear not', which are intended to reassure God's people that he is on their side. For example, through Isaiah God repeatedly told his people not to fear as 'I have made you, I have redeemed you, I have chosen you, I am with you, I will help you' (see Isa. 43:1, 5, 44:2). These promises mean we need not live in constant fear of something or someone else but that doesn't rule out the fear of the Lord as part of our relationship with God.

Having a true fear of the Lord releases many of his promises and gifts to us. One, which we mentioned above, is that the fear of the Lord is the beginning of wisdom. Here is the promise of a new mindset, one we would not naturally have. With the fear of the Lord as part of our overall perspective, we become wiser about God, life and ourselves. We begin to understand the world as it really is and get to know the ways and will of God better. It then becomes possible to denounce the ideas of the world and the musings of men as merely earthly wisdom, and to replace all this with the heavenly wisdom which God offers. The fear of the Lord sets us on the path of true wisdom and so protects us against deception, distortion and false teaching.

Another wonderful statement about the fear of the Lord is found in Isaiah 33:6. 'He will be the sure foundation for your times, a rich store of salvation and wisdom and knowledge; the fear of the LORD is the key to this treasure.'

There seems to be two ways of understanding this verse. One is that the fear of the Lord is in itself a treasure from him, but the alternative is that it is a key to a rich store of salvation, wisdom and knowledge. Who wouldn't want to open that treasury?!

There are many inspiring verses in scripture about the fear of the Lord. For instance, in Proverbs we read, 'Whoever fears the LORD has a secure fortress, and for their children it will be a refuge. The fear of the LORD is a fountain of life, turning a person from the snares of death' (Prov. 14:26-27). Later in Proverbs we are reassured that 'the fear of the LORD leads to life; then one rests content, untouched by trouble' (Prov. 19:23). And there are many more in the Psalms, too many to list here, so you will have to search them out for yourself!

We can learn more about the fear of the Lord by studying the history of Israel. When the Israelites were delivered from Egypt, they witnessed the saving power of God. It is recorded that 'when the Israelites saw the mighty hand of the LORD displayed against the Egyptians, the people feared the LORD and put their trust in him and in Moses his servant' (Exod. 14:31; also Deut. 10:20-21). The fear of the Lord was a natural response to this supernatural act. Previously they had been afraid of the Egyptians pursuing them and of the Red Sea in front of them. But once God had delivered them, this turned into a different fear, the fear of the Lord, which then led them to trust God more. There is a lesson here for us too. If we have known his saving power in our lives, we should no longer be frightened of our enemies behind us, but instead have the fear of the Lord who goes before us. We can then trust him to lead us further through life.

The Israelites next experienced the power of their God at Mount Sinai. This made them so afraid that they stayed at a distance and didn't want God to speak to them directly. Moses, on the other hand, approached the thick darkness where God was (Exod. 20:20-21). He no doubt did so in the fear of the Lord but he was no longer afraid. He had been afraid of God on a previous occasion, at the burning bush (Exod. 3:6), but now he knew God better he could get close enough to him to hear what he had to say to his people.

Being afraid of God is different from having the fear of the Lord. Being afraid means we run away, whereas the fear of the Lord draws us more into his presence. The Israelites were afraid of God and so held back. Moses had the fear of the Lord and so went into his presence. Having the fear of the Lord deepens our relationship with him, as does knowing his goodness towards us. God draws us closer to himself with two hands, goodness and fear, which work together to bring us into his presence. Once we know that God is good, then the fear of the Lord does not frighten us.

Also at Sinai, Moses told the Israelites, 'God has come to test you, so that the fear of God will be with you to keep you from sinning' (Exod. 20:20). The fear of the Lord was as important as the Law they were about to receive. Indeed, it was to work together with the laws to make them more effective. In Deut. 5:29, the fear of the Lord and obedience to him are linked when God says, 'Oh, that their hearts would be inclined to fear me and keep all my commands...'

The fear of God stops us from hiding sin in our hearts. It makes us want to steer clear of evil. In one of the wisdom books, we find that Job 'feared God and shunned evil' (Job 1:1). In all his troubles he never lost that fear of the Lord, which saw him through all his suffering and enabled him at the end to see God better (Job 42:5).

Another telling verse is Deuteronomy 10:12. Here Israel is asked, 'What does the Lord your God ask of you but to fear the Lord your God, to walk in obedience to him, to love him, to serve the LORD your God with all your heart and with all your soul.' We might expect God to require obedience, love and service, but it is noticeable that before all these comes the fear of the Lord as this acts as a motivation for the others.

Objections to the fear of the Lord still exist among some Christians who insist we should focus instead on God's love. They usually quote from 1 John 4:18 that 'perfect love drives out fear'. This is a common basis for ignoring the fear of the Lord or even for contradicting it. But this verse is referring to a certain kind of fear, that of punishment and judgement. The full sentence is, 'But perfect love drives out fear, because fear has to do with punishment.' The previous verse, verse 17, provides the context, which is about having confidence on the day of judgement. Believers don't fear the day of judgement because of God's love for us in taking on himself, in Christ, the punishment of our sins. This love drives out any fear of eternal punishment.

Others assert we are to think of ourselves as friends of God, and that friendship is inconsistent with fear. However, the two people in the Bible who are specifically called a friend of God also knew the fear of the Lord. One was Moses. In Exodus 33:11 we read, 'The LORD would speak to Moses face to face, as one speaks to a friend.' But we have already seen that he was also familiar with the fear of the Lord.

The other is Abraham, who is a called a friend of God three times in the Bible (2 Chr. 20:7, Isa. 41:8, Jas 2:23). But in Genesis 22:12, he is told, 'Now I know that you fear God, because you have not withheld from me your son, your only son.' In these cases, and also with us, fear and friendship can go together. They are not mutually exclusive.

Others might say this is all Old Testament. Isn't it different once we get to the New? Here are some verses that suggest otherwise.

Peter writes, 'Since you call on a Father who judges each person's work impartially, live out your time as foreigners here in reverent fear' (1 Pet. 1:17).

Paul tells the church at Corinth, 'Since, then, we know what it is to fear the Lord, we try to persuade others' (2 Cor. 5:11). Is Paul here suggesting that the fear of the Lord is a motivation for evangelism?

In the book of Acts the early church experienced the fear of the Lord from the beginning mainly due to the mighty works of God which were performed by the apostles (see Acts 2:43, 5:11).

Moreover, Jesus also taught his disciples to fear God. When telling them not to fear men who can only kill the body and after that can do no more, he continued, 'But I will show you whom you should fear: fear him who, after your body has been killed, has authority to throw you into hell. Yes, I tell you, fear him' (Luke 12:5).

A fear of men can enslave us and make us ineffective in serving God as we become more concerned about their opinions than with what God thinks or wants from us. This is the kind of fear Paul writes about in Romans 8:15 when he says, 'The Spirit you received does not make you slaves, so that you live in fear again.' God's Spirit sets us free from these wrong fears, so they do not control us or hold us back. The fear of the Lord is not like that. Rather it keeps us from compromising God's truth for personal gain, and enables us to esteem God's Word more than man's wisdom.

We have spent some time on this important topic as it is one of the bedrocks of wisdom in the biblical texts, and one of the least appreciated. In the next chapter we will consider another common word in the early chapter of Proverbs, namely 'son', and think how wisdom was passed on in Israelite society.

Chapter Three

Listen, My Son

In our exploration of biblical wisdom we are starting by examining one of the main wisdom books of the Old Testament, Proverbs. Within the overall structure of this book, chapters 1 to 9 are regarded as the first section, with 1:1-7 acting as a prologue not just to this portion but to the whole book. These seven verses set out the purpose and presuppositions of the book of Proverbs and highlight its distinctive concerns regarding the pursuit of wisdom. So it is not surprising to find that the motto phrase about the fear of the Lord, and in particular that 'the fear of the LORD is the beginning of wisdom', occurs at the climax of the prologue. Within Israelite society, not fearing God (in the way explained in our previous chapter) would be considered unwise.

While we acknowledge that taken together the first nine chapters form a complete section of the book, a fitting preparation for what is to follow, we also note that chapter 8 is a distinct poem and that chapter 9 is a fascinating study in its own right, so we will defer both of these to later in this book. Here, in this chapter, we will make some general observations which apply to chapters 1 to 9 as a whole, but when we pick out details, it will be from the first seven chapters only.

Overall, the opening nine chapters display some marked differences in comparison with the rest of the book, so much so that some scholars prefer not to regard their content as being actual proverbs. They argue it is not until 10:1 that the real collections of proverbs begin. But others insist that the description in 1:1 is very clear when it says, 'The proverbs of Solomon', especially as it uses exactly the same two Hebrew words as found in 10:1. It does seem unlikely that these two headings would mean significantly different things in their respective contexts so we should allow the term 'proverb' to cover all that we find in the entire book, including from the very start. This is especially so as the Hebrew word for 'proverb' (*mashal*) has a variety of meanings and is not restricted to the sort of terse two-liners that we find from chapter 10 onwards.

What is generally agreed is that chapters 1 to 9 are very different from the rest of the book in form and composition. The short snappy sayings which dominate later are noticeable by their absence and instead we have something that is more narrative in style. The arguments are more developed and the appeals more preachy. In that sense these opening chapters are more readable. In places they are like short essays whose aim is not to spoon feed via isolated sayings but to stimulate thought in various ways, using vivid pictures and analogies. The approach is to exhort and admonish, in readiness for the content to come from chapter 10 onwards, where there is usually no narrative thread, just collections of short statements mixed together with no apparent organisation. As such these later chapters are more difficult to read all at once. Rather, it seems we are to dip into them in the hope of landing on some appropriate 'bon mot'.

The narrative style of these opening chapters makes the book more accessible to begin with. Nevertheless, we do occasionally find something more proverbial encased with these brief essays. For instance, in 1:10-19, which is a warning against joining in with those whose aim is to get rich at the expense of others, there is a picturesque saying which is more in line with later proverbs: 'How useless to spread a net where every bird can see it' (1:17).

There is something similar in a later discourse. Proverbs 6:20-35 exposes the risks involved in sexual immorality. Tucked away in the centre of this mini lecture there are two striking questions. 'Can a man scoop fire into his lap without his clothes being burned? Can a man walk on hot coals without his feet being scorched?' (6:27-28). Here, neatly and graphically, the point is made. Warning given!

Overall these opening chapters employ various techniques, such as direct appeals, rhetorical questions, anecdotes and extended metaphors. The common factor in all this is the repeated phrase 'my son', which occurs eighteen times from 1:8 to 7:24 (sometimes in the plural, 'my sons'). This suggests these chapters reflect how a father is to instruct his son and explain the consequences of various actions, all within the general aim of shaping his son's character early in life. Not only was the fear of the Lord expected of every adult, but also that they would pass this on to the next generation (see Deut. 6:1-2, 20). The responsibility for the spiritual education of the young rested primarily within the family unit.

However, there is the additional point that 'son' is not necessarily a biological term. It can also refer to a student. We frequently see in scripture the teacher-student relationship described as father-son. So there is some debate whether this is not so much home-based instruction but that of professional sages within a school situation.

Often quoted here is Jeremiah 18:18, with its reference to 'the teaching of the law by the priest', 'counsel from the wise' and 'word from the prophets'. Some think this suggests there was a special category of officials within the royal court, called 'the wise', whose duty was to pass on wisdom. This may have been the case in other nations, such as Mesopotamia and Egypt, but there is little support in the Old Testament for this in Israelite culture. There is a hint in Ecclesiastes of a Teacher who was wise and also imparted knowledge to the people (Eccles. 12:9), but the idea that official groups of wisdom teachers were typical lacks any real evidence. It remains best to assume that teaching wisdom was primarily centred within the family and that proverbs such as these in chapters 1 to 7 were intended for a father to instruct his son in the general concepts of wisdom and to guide him in specific areas of life.

The household was the central unit of Old Testament Israel, socially, economically and spiritually. One role of the wisdom tradition was to preserve the wellbeing of the household, and many of the proverbs reflect this in the way they cover such matters as work and laziness, family life and relationships. It is not surprising, therefore, that chapters 1 to 7 are full of parental advice about seeing the world correctly and revealing the right way to walk through life.

The best *time* to learn wisdom is early in life, to prevent bad habits developing and to counter peer pressure. So naturally the best *place* to learn wisdom is in the home, within the family, where there can be both firmness and affection. Even if the parents were not specialist teachers, they could still pass on a wide variety of wisdom by engaging their children in the process of reciting, repeating and memorising. Proverbs are ideal for this and provide not just words for the mind but training for the character.

The instruction to memorise and store away wisdom in the heart is explicit in 3:1-4, which also displays a typical format for this section. An address (my son) leads to some imperatives or commands (in this case, the negative 'do not forget', and the positive 'store in your heart', v1). These are then followed by the promise of certain benefits designed to motivate compliance (long life, peace and prosperity, v2). This pattern is repeated in verses 3-4, where further directives (basically, to hold on to love and faithfulness) lead to more promises, this time of favour and a good name with God and men.

Storing wisdom in the heart is fundamental to the process of getting wise. Back in the very opening of the book it says that proverbs are given 'for gaining wisdom' (1:2). The Hebrew word used is *lada'at*, which comes from *yada*, meaning 'to know', but 'knowing wisdom' doesn't sound right, so 'gaining wisdom' seems a fair translation. It emphasises that this is not about knowledge or acquiring facts; nor is this primarily a cerebral activity, though of course it does involve mental processes. However, an even better translation would be that proverbs help us become *acquainted* with wisdom. This is the true meaning behind the Hebrew word 'to know'. The stress is on having an encounter. Wisdom is something we must get involved with at a personal level. We are to enter into a relationship with wisdom so that it directly impacts our lives. This also applies to those already wise and discerning so they can grow more and add to their wisdom (1:5). Proverbs provide valuable lessons throughout all of life.

Two other words stand out in the opening prologue. Proverbs 1:4 refers to those who are 'simple', and 1:7 mentions 'fools'. Both of these words recur frequently in Proverbs, so understanding their meaning is essential, especially as in neither case do they refer to any kind of mental deficiency or stupidity.

When someone in the biblical wisdom literature is described as simple it just means he is as yet untutored. He lacks wisdom not because he is slow-witted or dull-minded but solely because he is young, as indicated by the end of the second half of 1:4. This verse is an example of parallelism where the second part repeats the meaning of the first part but in slightly different words. So in biblical terms, simple equals young, and a simpleton is merely a person at the start of life. Like everyone at this stage he needs to be instructed in wisdom. He might still be rather naïve and gullible but he is not necessarily reluctant when it comes to hearing words from the wise.

By contrast, if a simple person needs instruction, a fool needs correction. He has already heard the words of the wise but rejected them. He prefers to ignore wisdom and go his own way. Just as biblical wisdom is not primarily about intelligence so, biblically, folly does not equate to stupidity or being 'intellectually challenged', as we might say today.

Someone is a fool not because he lacks intelligence but because he chooses to leave God out of any situation. Indeed, out of his life entirely. As the psalmist writes, 'The fool says in his heart, "There is no God"' (Ps. 14:1). If you believe there is no God, then you can't ask him for wisdom. A fool is literally God-less. As a result he makes bad choices and his life suffers and withers. He fails through moral deficiency. This is why folly is so widespread today, even among the cleverest of people. You may have noticed this!

Wisdom is about how to live life well and handle situations properly. A foolish person wastes his life, while a wise person makes the best use of whatever life throws at him. A fool is someone who has not learned to live life in the way most beneficial for himself or pleasing to God. He might be highly intelligent but he can also be self-centred and obstinate, so placing himself beyond whatever help true wisdom from God could bring him.

Making the right choice is central to biblical wisdom teaching. The rewards of choosing correctly are great but discipline is needed if these are to be achieved. The purpose of the opening chapters of Proverbs is to prepare a young person to receive and accept the traditional wisdom of Israel, and if necessary to persuade him that he really needs it.

Much of this traditional wisdom is found in the rest of the book of Proverbs, from chapter 10 onwards. But before we examine these chapters, we first have an appointment with a special lady.

It is time to meet Lady Wisdom and see what she offers.

Chapter Four

Meet Lady Wisdom

So far, the opening chapters of the book of Proverbs have introduced us to the key idea of 'the fear of the LORD' and to the fact that within Israelite society fatherly advice was deemed necessary to give young people a good start in life. We have also seen that just as wisdom is not about being clever or intelligent, folly does not equate to stupidity or being 'intellectually challenged', as we might say these days. Rather a fool is someone who leaves God out of the situation entirely. As a result he makes bad choices.

The book of Proverbs starts off by addressing those at a stage in life when they must decide the direction they will go in. It is easy to lose sight of this main point in all the minutiae of the many proverbs that follow. This need for correct decision making is often expressed in terms of various dualisms. For example there are two paths to choose between in 4:18-19, the path of the righteous and the way of the wicked. Then there is a choice between two houses to visit in chapter 9, which we will look at in detail in our next chapter. But above all, we come across two possible female companions, Lady Wisdom and Dame Folly, not named as such in the text but commonly identified in this way. The contrast between them is apparent early on. For instance, wisdom will love and protect you and give you a crown for your head (4:6-9), while the alternative is compared to an adulterous woman full of deception who leads you to death (5:3-8). Here is the real choice to be made for a young man at the start of his journey in life.

After several chapters of fatherly advice, the attention switches to Wisdom herself. She is given voice and character in two dramatic chapters: chapter 8, which will occupy our attention now, and chapter 9 to come next. But before we come to these specific chapters, we should note that we meet Lady Wisdom several times beforehand.

Our first introduction to her is in 1:20-33, where in similar vein to chapter 8, she is calling out in public places to all who will listen. Her impassioned pleas are specifically made to the simple and to fools, hence our need to define them carefully in our previous chapter. Her desire is made clear in verse 23, 'Then I will pour out my thoughts to you, I will make known to you my teachings.' But her frustration is also on display. The simple remain simple, and the fools hate what she has to offer. They disregard her and so are heading for disaster, though she remains hopeful, ending with, 'Whoever listens to me will live in safety and be at ease, without fear of harm' (v33).

Lady Wisdom is mentioned again in 3:13-18, this time indirectly rather than through her own direct speech. Here, her attractiveness is spelled out through the benefits and bounty that she offers.

Another reference is in 7:4, where we are invited to talk to Lady Wisdom in a cordial and welcoming manner, as if we were wanting to strike up a close relationship with her. 'Say to wisdom, "You are my sister," and to insight, "You are my relative."' We mentioned before that the purpose of these proverbs, and therefore of the book as whole, is that we should get acquainted with wisdom, to relate to it personally, not just know it. Here the same point is made. We are to treat wisdom like a close family member.

All these previous references prepare us for a more concentrated expression of the nature of wisdom which is to come in chapter 8. Here we find one of the great poems of the wisdom literature, indeed of the Old Testament as a whole. This magnificent poetic declaration of wisdom is delivered through the literary technique known as personification. Closely related to metaphor, personification is the assigning of human qualities, abilities or actions to a non-personal thing or entity. In this case, personification is chosen as a particularly effective means of communicating graphically the importance of wisdom, how it operates in human affairs and the benefits it brings. So in both this chapter and the next, there is a sustained personification of wisdom. Indeed in chapter 9 the personification is extended to her main rival, Folly, in order to demonstrate a complete contrast between the two. This will occupy our next chapter. Meanwhile, here we examine in some detail this remarkable eighth chapter of Proverbs.

Nearly the whole chapter is given over to Lady Wisdom's own words. After the introductory three verses to grab our attention and provide a fictional but nonetheless realistic setting for her speech, she is allowed to address us herself. She shows herself to be a skilled orator and an authoritative preacher.

Her opening words in verses 4-11 are a commanding invitation to listen to her. We are summoned into her presence as she has something very important to tell us. She calls out to all humanity but especially, as we have seen before, to those who are still simple, or lacking instruction, and to those still foolish enough to deny or reject the wisdom they have been offered. She demands to be heard, confident that what she says is true and just. Those who are discerning will realise this, but those who are not, will go astray. The consequences are clear, as is the need to make the right choice. 'Choose my instruction' is her plea.

In verses 12-14 Wisdom continues to proclaim her qualities and strengths. She dwells with prudence. She has sound judgement, insight and power. We also find in verse 13 another reference to fearing the Lord, but this time the phrase does not say this is the beginning of wisdom (perhaps this is less appropriate from the mouth of wisdom herself) but rather that this will enable us to hate evil just as she does. Once the fear of the Lord has led us to begin a journey through life with her, then its continuing influence results in sharing her values.

In the next section, verses 15-21, more of Wisdom's attributes and benefits are described, together with a new focus that those in high office, such as kings and rulers, need her if they are to govern successfully. If this is true of them, then why not for the rest of us?

Fascinating as it is to hear Lady Wisdom extol her own virtues in this way, it is the next section, verses 22-31, that is the most illuminating and thought-provoking. At this point, the poem takes us into a new realm of mystery and contemplation as Wisdom's origin and place at the start of creation is revealed. Wisdom is shown as having existed before creation as we know it. Moreover, she was 'brought forth' as the first of all God's creative works (v22). There is some debate over this verse as the word for 'brought forth' could be translated as 'possessed' or 'acquired', but it is perfectly plausible to think in terms of Wisdom having been birthed or begotten, especially as later, in verses 24 and 25, she declares, 'I was given birth.'

In a remarkable collection of statements we are being offered a mystical vision. A series of 'before' clauses in verses 23-26 stress that Wisdom existed prior to anything else in creation. Equally amazing is the following string of 'when' clauses in verses 27-29, which speak of her presence at the very moments when the Lord brought everything else into existence. Overall, this is a very special part of the book of Proverbs and indeed of scripture in general. However, we need to make some further clarification regarding the actual status and role of Lady Wisdom as outlined in these verses.

Firstly, this passage is not suggesting that Lady Wisdom is herself divine, part of the Godhead, or eternally pre-existent. We may be tempted to think ahead to the New Testament and what we are told there about Christ or the Holy Spirit, but here the writer is clearly personifying a concept not describing a personality. This comes out earlier in Proverbs, such as 3:19-20, which shows that wisdom is an attribute of God and not a figure that stands in equality with him.

Secondly, Lady Wisdom is not described as being actively engaged in making the world. Rather she was at God's side as he went about his creative activity (8:30). We could, however, argue from this passage that creation was formed with her at the forefront of God's mind, and that her presence made a difference to the outcome, but we should always bear in mind that she is a personified attribute of God not an independent person. Perhaps one way of reading this passage is to say that creation came from a wise God, that it was put together in a wise way, and that when he spoke everything into being it was with words of wisdom.

One translation of verse 30, often found in the footnote, replaces the phrase 'I was *constantly* at his side' with 'I was the *master worker* at his side' (or even *a little child* at his side). Calling her a master worker could suggest that Wisdom did indeed participate in creating our world, at least in some capacity, but to press this too far would be at odds with the chapter as a whole, including the rest of verses 30-31 where Wisdom is delighting and rejoicing in what is happening in front of her. The impression is that she had a front-row seat enjoying watching God going about his creative work, and a better translation would be, 'I was so close to God in his role as a master workman.'

Although we should not insist on any kind of pre-figuring of Christ in this passage, or assume that the New Testament relies upon these verses to build what might be called a wisdom Christology, it is clear that the language and imagery in Proverbs 8 has great depths and insights which, once we have knowledge of the incarnation, can be said to find even greater fulfilment in the New Testament. Meanwhile we can enjoy it on its own terms. Here is God's own personal wisdom, contained within himself but brought forth in a special way as he expressed himself in the joys of creating our world.

The overall aim of chapter 8 is to bolster Wisdom's authority and intensify our readiness to listen to her. Wisdom as an impersonal entity offers the same benefits as the personified account, and both preserve us from the same perils. These effects are described in almost identical words in both formats, but the personified form may attract some who would otherwise dismiss these words of wisdom. In addition, as we shall see in Proverbs chapter 9, this allows the contrast with folly to be developed to a greater extent.

Meanwhile there is a need for an immediate response. 'Now then, my children, listen to me' (v32). In the closing section of the chapter the tone reverts to something familiar. We find the same promises of prosperity and threats of harm. But in the light of what we have just read, not to respond positively to Wisdom is even more dangerous. It is to choose our own unmaking and deny our very own life.

Chapters 8 and 9 crown the opening section of the book of Proverbs. The praise of Wisdom reaches a climax of eloquence and urgency. Her person merges with her teachings. To possess her is not some mystical experience but a way of listening to truth.

Before we leave this chapter, it is worth noting there are similar poems elsewhere in the wisdom books. One is in the apocryphal book the Wisdom of Ben Sirach, chapter 24, where Wisdom again speaks directly to us in self-praise. She also declares, 'I came forth from the mouth of the Most High' (v3) and, 'Before the ages, in the beginning, he created me' (v9). The similarities with Proverbs chapter 8 are striking.

We find a similar personification of Wisdom in another apocryphal book, the Wisdom of Solomon chapters 7 to 8, where she is portrayed as the one that Solomon sought as his bride. And there is another great wisdom poem in Job chapter 28, which we will be studying later but is worth reading now, as are the apocryphal ones mentioned above if you can find them easily.

But meanwhile, in our next chapter we will continue our study of Lady Wisdom in Proverbs 9, where we must also be prepared to meet another female character of a very different kind.

Chapter Five

A Tale of Two Houses

In our last chapter we looked at the magnificent wisdom poem found in Proverbs 8 and heard from Lady Wisdom herself as she extolled her virtues and explained her origins and place at the start of creation.

After this we might expect chapter 9 to be an anti-climax, but far from it. This chapter is equally impressive, though different in style. We continue to hear from Lady Wisdom but now have to contend with her rival, usually referred to as Dame Folly, though Madame Folly might be more appropriate. She displays all the fatal charms of a whore and adulteress, in contrast to the figure of Lady Wisdom as our true soulmate and bride.

The idea of personification, which we met in the last chapter, continues as Lady Wisdom and Dame Folly compete with each other to determine the fate of each generation. We should remind ourselves that personification is a literary device which assigns human abilities, qualities or actions to a non-personal thing or entity. It is designed to speak more directly to us but without raising the 'character' to the level of a personality or giving it the status of deity. The personification of Wisdom aims to persuade us that what is on offer in these pages is above and beyond human instruction or clever thoughts; here we have not just piecemeal snippets of advice on isolated topics but an integrated coherent worldview. This is about getting into the mind of the maker, thinking his thoughts after him.

It would be a good idea at this point to pause and read the whole of chapter 9 out loud. You could dramatise it using different 'voices'. In this way the structure of the chapter should become clear. It is arranged symmetrically in three groups of six verses each, with the first six and the last six providing a series of contrasts. The central six verses act as an interlude to heighten the tension and remind us of the implications of our decision to follow Wisdom or Folly by offering character sketches of those who belong to the two opposing camps.

Sharp contrasts and vivid comparisons are key features of the book of Proverbs. Indeed it largely teaches by contrasts, so as you read look out for four of these: the houses, the appeals, the meals, and the destinies. We will examine each of these in turn next.

Firstly, the two houses. As rival hostesses, Wisdom and Folly seek to entice passers-by to enter their respective houses. Wisdom has built her own house and fashioned it herself. The seven pillars (which, incidentally, is the origin of the phrase 'the seven pillars of wisdom') suggest the inner court of a well-to-do house. The overall impression is one of spaciousness and stability. Moreover, the number seven signifies completeness or perfection; her house lacks nothing. It is also fully equipped and staffed with willing servants ready to assist.

We learnt in 8:12 that Wisdom dwells together with Prudence. Whether she is one of these servants or a permanent house guest isn't specified. We might prefer to think of her more as a companion than a servant, but perhaps she helps around the house too! We also know from the previous chapter that Wisdom is stated to be the first of God's creative works (8:22-30). She then watched God construct the rest of creation, gaining knowledge and insights into the mind of the creator at work. Her own house would therefore be built in harmony with all that God had made. We can be confident that it will be secure and enduring, founded on eternal principles and purposes.

Folly's house may seem pleasantly situated on the heights with a good view over the city (9:14) but there is no mention that she has built this herself or that it is pleasant in any way. But given that her guests are described as being 'deep in the realm of the dead' (v18) it seems in reality she lives in the depths, inhabiting a dark and dingy underworld. Her house is more like a den, intended to attract nocturnal lowlife, and cannot compare in any way with the palatial splendour and elegance of her rival's house.

This initial contrast of the two houses challenges us to find our true home. Which threshold will we cross? Where will we settle? In particular, the setting of a house forms an appropriate starting point for comparing the relative merits of Wisdom and Folly for, as we have seen earlier, in Jewish society wisdom begins at home. Children are to be instructed within the family circle, and family life is founded upon the wisdom passed down through the generations.

The next contrast between Lady Wisdom and Dame Folly involves the words they speak, and the appeals they make.

Both seem to call out in identical fashion to entice guests into their houses. The same words are used in both verse 4 and verse 16, but their approaches are very different. Wisdom is more active, taking the initiative. She busies herself beforehand, preparing her meal with thought and care. She sends out her servants and then she goes out herself to make sure that as many as possible hear her invitation. She goes to the highest point of the city (which, we've seen, is where Folly lives) so that she can be heard by everyone. She proclaims her message to one and all, seeking their attention.

Folly's appeal is also earnest and pressing but she simply sits at home and shouts out to those who pass by (v13-15). There are various ways to describe how Folly tries to appeal to passers-by. She is loud, clamorous, brash and vulgar. Overall, the picture is that of the glossy allure of a prostitute. She sits slovenly in her doorway, unruly, like a harlot on display.

While Folly sits back, Wisdom again shares the heart of God, going after the lost. She operates purposefully towards a clear goal. Her appeal is urgent but gracious. But Folly is not creative. She cannot build her own house or think of her own words. She merely mimics Wisdom's cry and then adds what is probably a popular saying of the time: 'Stolen water is sweet; food eaten in secret is delicious!' (v17). Though without an original thought in her head, her manner can still coax and flatter. Would we find this kind of talk tempting?

As we've said before, the 'simple' mentioned in both verse 4 and verse 16 are those still uncommitted, yet to set foot in either house. They are passing by and so still open to persuasion. Both Wisdom and Folly are contending to take them into their own house before the other does. But notice how in verse 13 Folly herself is also described as simple and ignorant. She is seeking the company of others of her own kind!

The third contrast is over the quite different meals the two hostesses offer. Wisdom provides a sumptuous banquet, having taken time and trouble. She has prepared her meat, in itself a rare luxury. She has probably killed and dressed the animals herself. She has mixed her wine, possibly mingling it with honey and spices to bring out the best in its flavour. Overall, this is a special treat. Wisdom can say come and eat 'my food' (v5), whereas Folly is again unable to provide anything of this kind herself. Her food is 'stolen' (v17). Yet how tempting can forbidden fruit appear to be!

The meal imagery is powerful. Accepting food and coming to someone's table creates a special kind of fellowship, binding people together. Sharing food even has a covenantal aspect. For instance, at communion or the Lord's Supper, we participate in God's meal, the bread and wine he has lovingly prepared and at such a cost. What does the world have to offer instead? Folly's food has no real sustenance for she is not prepared to pay a price in providing it.

It is with the fourth contrast that the chapter reaches its full impact. Here we discover the ultimate outcome of the choice of house. Two different destinies are at stake. Wisdom offers life (v6); Folly offers death (v18). In verse 18 the realm of the dead is Sheol, the usual Hebrew word for the shadowy existence beyond the grave, whereas the word for 'the dead' is *rephaim*, literally 'shades' or 'shadows', but typically referring to departed spirits. It matters not whether we think of her guests as actually dead or just metaphorically so. They are already on the path towards death. Real life is absent in her house. In fact, a sense of doom pervades the whole dwelling place.

There is little of substance in anything Folly provides. Her food does not do what food should do, namely bring life. To enter Folly's house and dine from her table is to depart from true living long before physical death makes its claim. The hopelessness of the situation is compounded by the fact that those who enter do not realise what is happening to them. They cannot tell what they are missing. Because they are foolish they do not think too deeply. For them, ignorance is bliss! The sensations of the moment are sufficient. Thus Folly serves them well. All cares about the future are dispelled. They do not have to watch their step for they are going nowhere.

Wisdom can offer life as her very existence comes from the Author of Life himself (see 8:35). She rejoices in that life and in her God-given role to encourage us to live well. Eating with her means we walk in the way of insight (9:6). We realise how life works and how to gain its rewards. With Wisdom we walk in understanding; with Folly, we sit in ignorance.

Our choice of Wisdom or Folly as a dinner partner has profound implications for the whole of life and beyond. Gaining wisdom is not merely the gradual accumulation of skills and knowledge but a life-and-death, hearts-and-minds struggle between opposing principles which affects not just life here and now, but also our eternal destiny.

We should also note that there are only two houses to choose between, not a whole street full. There is no middle way or neutral ground between Wisdom and Folly, no varying shades of opinion between. If we do not accept Wisdom's offer then Folly will grab us.

This sharp contrast also occurs in the New Testament and in particular in the teaching of Jesus. For instance, he talks of two gates and two paths (Matt. 7:13-14). One leads to life, the other to destruction. He also teaches a memorable parable of two houses, one built on rock by a wise man, the other on sand by a foolish man (Matt. 7:24-27). One provides security, the other leads to disaster.

Proverbs chapter 9 presses home the advice given in the earlier chapters of the book. It does so via the simplicity of a cartoon sketch of rival hostesses inviting us to their very different feasts of life or death. Its climax of a knife-edge choice and sense of dread for the man who chooses wrongly, provides a keen incentive for taking seriously what we have heard so far. But equally this chapter acts as a prelude to the anthology of sayings that follow. We are left in no doubt as to the vital importance of what is still to come.

By this point in the book of Proverbs we realise we are being provided with the very embodiment of the rules by which creation operates and which must be followed if life is to be fruitful and fulfilling. The wise man discovers a delight in Wisdom's heavenly origin and continual intimate relationship with God. He rejoices that her clean living and high principles make her a suitable companion for the journey through life and quest for a closer walk with God.

After all the fatherly advice in Proverbs, it has made a change to hear from a female character in Lady Wisdom. We commented in an earlier chapter that the Hebrew for wisdom, *hokmah*, is a feminine word. One aspect of this might be to encourage young men to pursue wisdom as they would pursue women, and to seek her with as much thought as they would a life partner. In the final chapter of Proverbs we will meet two more female characters, the mother of a king and a noble wife. But before then we have several collections of proverbial sayings to think about, specifically those of King Solomon, starting with Proverbs chapter 10.

Chapter Six

Proverbs: The Collections

So far we have covered the first nine chapters of the book of Proverbs, which concludes with a magnificent wisdom poem in chapter 8 and a contest in chapter 9 between Lady Wisdom and Dame Folly as they attempt to win the hearts and minds of those who 'pass by' their respective houses, wondering which one to enter.

As we move into chapter 10, the style changes completely. We now find what we usually think of as 'proverbs'. Rather than the mini essays and poetry of the previous chapters we have an anthology of short disparate sayings. We shall examine the nature and style of these in our next chapter. For now we will focus on outlining the rest of the book and describing what is there in general terms.

Proverbs is not a normal book. Nor is it just a collection of proverbs. Rather it is a collection of collections, some attributed to Solomon, some to others. The overall composition of the book from chapter 10 onwards is usually summarised as follows.

The first main collection is ascribed to Solomon and extends from 10:1 to 22:16. The next section runs from 22:17 to the end of chapter 24 and is generally referred to as 'the sayings of the wise'. After this comes another collection of proverbs of Solomon, which occupies chapters 25 to 29. Chapter 30 contains the sayings of Agur, who intriguingly is a non-Israelite, while the final chapter splits into two sections: the sayings of King Lemuel (another non-Israelite) in the first nine verses and an epilogue in verses 10 to 31, which is another poem, this time extolling the virtues and character of a noble wife.

We will explore these various collections separately and in more detail later, but now we will draw out a few points from each in order to get a fuller picture of the book of Proverbs as a whole.

The first main collection (10:1–22:16) contains around 375 proverbs under the heading 'The proverbs of Solomon'. We noted before that this phrase occurs at the start of the book (1:1). Perhaps this is just a reminder or it may be indicating that what we have read so far is not actually by Solomon and now they start properly. Here we find the sort of sayings that he is famous for. Notice that this phrase occurs again at 25:1: 'These are more proverbs of Solomon.' This starts what is known as Solomon's second collection, which follows a smaller section of sayings that are clearly stated as being from other wise men (22:17). So in 25:1 we are told we are returning to Solomon. Here are some more by him. Perhaps 10:1 acts in a similar fashion.

But are they really *'by* Solomon' anyway? What does *'of'* mean in this context? Did they originate with Solomon, actually written by him, or did he merely collect them? Because of Solomon's fame regarding wisdom it is reasonably assumed that he did produce them himself.

In support of this, one verse often quoted is 1 Kings 4:32, part of a passage about his great wisdom which mentions 3,000 proverbs. However, what is often missed is that it simply says he spoke (or uttered) them, which leaves the matter of their origin unclear. Solomon may still have been deemed wise if he had collected them from others, learnt them by heart, and then spoken them out at the right time. His application of them might be where his wisdom was shown. However, it is still possible, even likely, that he did write them himself, though in the ancient world the wisdom contained within a proverb was considered more important than the proverb's authorship. The same applies to other works of wisdom, as we shall discuss later in this book. But for now we can readily accept that these proverbs are from Solomon himself. Even so, the 800 or so that appear in Proverbs is only a selection from his complete output of 3,000, though it is a sizeable proportion of the approximately 900 proverbs found in the book as a whole.

From chapter 10 to the end, with the exception of the final poem (31:10-31), there is little or no systematic ordering to the proverbs within the various collections. Attempts to find an overall structure have proved futile so it remains best to regard each collection as a largely unconnected series of one-liners, with very little continuity or flow of thought. As such, each proverb can be savoured on its own, though occasionally we may think a proverb has been intentionally set next to its neighbour. Indeed some do seem to be paired on the basis of semantics or syntax or a common theme. Moreover, it is possible to find some larger topical groupings, such as in 16:10-15 and 25:2-7, with repeated references to 'the king' or kings generally, which suggests some kind of deliberate clustering. But by and large we can regard each proverb as self-contained and randomly placed.

Another feature worth mentioning at this point is how the two parts of a proverb can be linked. In some cases there is a 'but' in the middle; in others, the joining word is 'and'. There are technical terms for these, which we will mention again in the next chapter. For now, we simply note that those with a 'but' set up a contrast and that these feature strongly in chapters 10 to 15, the first half of Solomon's first collection. However, they do also occur in the remaining chapters of this collection, so at best this indicates a rather loose form of editing rather than any definitive principle of arrangement.

We have already seen that the second collection of Solomon opens in 25:1 with 'These are more proverbs of Solomon'. But this sentence continues with 'compiled by the men of Hezekiah king of Judah'. We shall discuss this more in a later chapter but for now this verse emphasises that Proverbs is a composite work put together over a long period of time. Even if the first collection of Solomon was published during or just after his reign, this part of Proverbs must have been compiled over 200 years later, during the time of Hezekiah. Some think this provides a decisive date for the completed version of Proverbs but others argue this was just another step on the way towards the final edition, which may not have appeared until after the exile. Under this theory, the final revision was probably undertaken by Ezra who, because of his skill as a scribe and teacher, is often associated with such projects! But it clearly doesn't matter to us when the book of Proverbs was completed or how long it took for this to happen. The wisdom in it is timeless and not directly related to any particular historical setting.

A further point of interest derives from the section that occurs between the two Solomon collections, and which is described in 22:17 as 'The sayings of the wise', or, in some Bibles, as 'Thirty Sayings of the Wise'. It is generally regarded by scholars that this portion of Proverbs resembles, in many ways, an ancient Egyptian wisdom document from around 1200 BC entitled 'The Instruction of Amenemope' (or Amenemopet). The content and verbal similarities are quite striking, so much so that experts are convinced that some affinity between the teaching of Amenemope and the proverbs in 22:17 to 24:22 is indisputable. So what are we to make of this? How explicit is the relationship between them? Did one 'borrow' from the other or is there a third common source?

Then, as mentioned above, the last two chapters of Proverbs are definitely non-Israelite in origin, usually taken to be from Arabian sources. Altogether the inclusion within the Hebrew Scriptures of wisdom from outside of Israel raises many questions. For instance, we might wonder if this reduces the inspiration of scripture. Can these passages still be the Word of God? And how do these proverbs relate to Israel's covenant faith with Yahweh? Did the compiler of Proverbs make allowances or alterations which would enable them to qualify for inclusion? Perhaps he only selected those which seemed to fit fairly well and wouldn't cause too much of a stir.

But the real question is, why should we be surprised at all that the Bible adopts wisdom from external ancient sources? After all, the wisdom literature is less ethnically based or culturally specific than much of the rest of the Old Testament. It has a more international flavour and applicability. Indeed, it may be argued that there is a form of universal wisdom common to all mankind, similar to that of common grace, which is independent of any particular belief in God. As well as specific grace for salvation based on faith, God looks after all mankind when, for example, he causes the sun to shine and rain to fall on both the righteous and the unrighteous (see Matt. 5:45).

Overall, it would be rash to claim that wisdom was confined only to God's covenant people. All nations sought to uncover a sense of order within the universe and to address common issues of need and concern within human existence. It is therefore to be expected that many similarities would be found within the wisdom texts of the various people groups throughout the then known world.

So it is no surprise that, when it came to wisdom, Israel showed a greater openness to other nations than they did in other areas of their life and faith. They were more prepared to incorporate into their own literature what they found elsewhere. However, this did not mean they simply plagiarised the wisdom of other nations or took it on board wholesale. Modification was required to shape it to fit their own distinctive faith in Yahweh and their understanding of covenant redemption. This also meant rejecting certain features and assumptions of the wisdom of other nations. For instance, Egypt thought of wisdom as a goddess in its own right, which is not the same as the personification of wisdom we met earlier. So by careful selection and adaptation, Israel was able to embrace the wisdom of other nations while retaining an orientation towards its own traditions, belief system and experiences of God.

We also note that it would not have been particularly difficult for the Israelites to come into contact with the wisdom material of other nations and regions, such as Edom, Tyre, Persia, and most notably Egypt and the Mesopotamian empires of Assyria and Babylon. Israel's history often overlapped with many of these.

For example, Egypt's wisdom tradition is known to be very old, dating back to the third millennium BC. This was long before Israel existed but their link with this came early in their own history through none other than Moses. We know from Exodus 2:1-11 that Moses was brought up in the Egyptian court having been rescued by Pharaoh's own daughter. Moreover, Stephen's speech in Acts chapter 7 records that Moses was 'educated in all the wisdom of the Egyptians' (Acts 7:22). Here was Moses tapping into an already well-established wisdom as part of his preparation for the work God had for him. But we also see in Hebrews 11:24 that Moses 'refused to be known as the son of Pharaoh's daughter'. Although he learnt from the wisdom of Egypt, Moses didn't want to assimilate completely, choosing instead to retain his identity as a Hebrew.

It is also known that schools of wisdom flourished in both Egypt and Mesopotamia from the third millennium BC onwards. Here scribes copied out instructions to be handed down from father to son on topics such as truth, integrity, generosity, self-control, speech and silence. The emphasis was on the need to listen and obey. This would lead to success and prosperity in life as well as inner harmony and integration with others and the world around. All this is very similar to what we have already seen in the opening chapters of Proverbs.

Solomon's reign was a time of expanding horizons within Israel's history. He built a large navy and increased trade with other nations. This resulted not just in an exchange of goods but also in culture and ideas. God may have given special wisdom to Solomon but it was only in comparison with the wisdom of all the people of the East and of Egypt that it became clear just how wise he was (1 Kgs 4:29-31). He outshone them all, but that didn't mean there wasn't shared wisdom between nations, or that the wisdom of others was worthless.

Now that we have gained an overview of the book of Proverbs, we are ready to examine the nature and style of the individual proverb. Next we will examine what makes a proverb, a proverb.

Chapter Seven

Proverbs: Their Nature and Style

So far in our examination of the book of Proverbs we have looked in detail at the first nine chapters and outlined the various collections in the rest of the book. We now turn our attention to how an individual proverb encapsulates wisdom and delivers it to us. We will ask: what makes a proverb, a proverb? How should we read a proverb in order to gain access to that wisdom? Here is a specific literary genre which demands its own set of interpretative rules. If proverbs are to be understood correctly we need to take on board these principles.

We should start with a definition of the word 'proverb'. In Hebrew this is *mashal*, which is derived from a word meaning 'to be like' or 'to resemble'. Hence the main purpose of a proverb is to make a comparison, which is the approach Jesus often used in his mini parables when, for instance, he began by saying, 'What is the kingdom of God like? What shall I compare it to?' (Luke 13:18-19). In technical terms, a proverb acts as a similitude, which means that one thing, or one course of action, is set alongside another to show what it is really like or to highlight potential consequences. Thus the form of a proverb is more likely to be a short saying with one clear and obvious point than an extensive reflection containing development of thought. In addition, we should bear in mind that a proverb can also accentuate differences as well as similarities.

As we explore the characteristics of a proverb, let's first determine what a proverb is and then, just as important, what it is not.

First and foremost, a proverb is poetry. Ancient wisdom largely communicated its message via poetry, so it is not surprising that most biblical wisdom literature is poetic in style. But although there is much in common with English poetry, we must be aware that Hebrew poetry has its own distinctive features and peculiarities.

A biblical proverb is usually (but not always) in the form of a couplet where the aim is not to rhyme words but thought and meaning. It employs rhythm (or metre) rather than rhyme. Other techniques include alliteration (where words start with the same letter, such as look and leap) and assonance, which is similar to rhyme, where a resemblance is formed through repeated vowel sounds (such as nine and time). All these act as aids to memory. Indeed, the English words used above as examples may have reminded you of something!

However, the main distinctive feature of Hebrew poetry in general, and hence regularly found in proverbs, is known as parallelism. This is a literary device in which the second line completes the first line in one of three ways. It can echo or reinforce the first line. This is called synonymous parallelism and here the link word between the lines is 'and'. Alternatively, the second line can contrast the first line, using 'but', though sometimes the link word is 'better'. This is known as antithetical parallelism. Then there is the less common form of parallelism known as synthetic or progressive in which the second line develops the thought of the first line, taking it a step further. Here the link word is usually 'for', though 'and' can be used instead.

We mentioned this idea of parallelism briefly in our previous chapter where we said that proverbs with 'but' in the middle occur a great deal in chapters 10 to 15. Here are some examples of these antithetical or contrasting proverbs:

'A wise son brings joy to his father, but a foolish son brings grief to his mother' (10:1).

'The LORD detests dishonest scales, but accurate weights find favour with him' (11:1).

'A gentle answer turns away wrath, but a harsh word stirs up anger' (15:1). Notice the two sets of contrasts, one between 'gentle answer' and 'harsh word', and the other between 'turns away' and 'stirs up'.

Here is another, this time from the second collection by Solomon:

'Blessed is the one who always trembles before God, but whoever hardens their heart falls into trouble' (28:14).

As for a synthetic or progressive proverb, where the second part develops or heightens the meaning of the first, 16:31 says, 'Grey hair is a crown of splendour; it is attained in the way of righteousness.'

An example of a synonymous proverb where the second part reinforces the first would be, 'My son, do not despise the LORD's discipline, and do not resent his rebuke' (3:11). We also note that the next verse, 3:12, continues the thought in a progressive way, building further upon verse 11 by adding, 'because the LORD disciplines those he loves, as a father the son he delights in'.

Further features of a proverb include being pithy and picturesque. Using a few well-chosen words a proverb aims to quickly sketch a picture in the mind. It draws on vivid imagery and figurative language to delight our imagination and create something memorable. For instance, after the rather prosaic statement in 1:8 about listening to instruction and not forsaking teaching, we are treated to the delightful imagery that such wisdom is like a garland to grace the head and a chain to adorn the neck (1:9).

Another glorious example is that a ruling rightly given is 'like apples of gold in settings of silver' (25:11). And who can forget the images of a sluggard turning in his bed like a creaky door on its hinges or a quarrelsome wife dripping like a leaky roof in a storm (26:14, 27:15)?

As for being pithy, a proverb is designed to get to the point quickly. After all, a proverb is a saying, not a dissertation or three-point sermon. It employs an economy of expression, with its language stripped down to essentials for maximum impact and memorability. As someone once said, a proverb is 'an adage without paddage'.

Such brevity is typical of the wisdom of the ancient Near East at the time, and of folk wisdom in general. This is also a feature of English proverbs. Just think of some yourself and you'll soon realise this.

Proverbs: Their Nature and Style

Proverbs employ crisp turns of phrase. They provide nuggets of wisdom within compressed statements that are artfully crafted to be striking, thought-provoking and memorable. They are tailored in such a way that once heard, you cannot get them out of your head. It therefore takes great skill to compose a proverb, but when done well the results are impressive, effective and long-lasting.

However, this bite-size wisdom is not merely intellectual fast food. Proverbs are intended to be very practical. Here is real life at work. So they need to be chewed over, savoured and relished, not just swallowed whole in one go before moving on to something else. The brevity of a proverb is appealing, but its larger message needs to be unpacked over time.

Now we come to what a proverb is not, what it cannot do given that it is poetic in style, imaginative by nature and brief in form.

Firstly, because a proverb is not a lengthy narrative it cannot be expected to be comprehensive in what it offers. In a particular situation or set of circumstances a proverb provides some pertinent wisdom rather than a complete answer.

In addition, proverbs are not absolute truths or universal laws, so they do not have to be true all the time. They are usually true, or at least quite often, but at times there will be exceptions to what they say. Try this for yourself. Pick a biblical proverb at random and see if you think it should always be true.

The fact that there can be exceptions to what a proverb is telling us means we may feel let down at times when a proverb 'doesn't work'. What we need to understand is that the advice offered by a proverb is based upon observation and generalisation. It comes from a long and purposeful look at life and the world around us. From this emerges some guidance in summarised form which indicates how things usually work out, or how they should work out once the right path is taken. But this is not always going to be the case. Life is more complicated than anything these minimalistic sayings can propose.

It has rightly been said that a proverb is a short sentence founded upon long experience. Once we realise this is how a proverb is produced, and how it operates, then we can benefit from its contribution towards our understanding of the world and find it helpful when we need to choose well in confusing or ambiguous circumstances. But we should always beware of making a huge life decision solely on the basis of a single proverb.

From what we have said so far, it should also be clear that proverbs are not promises. There are no guarantees attached. This is another important point. It means we cannot complain if a proverb doesn't turn out as we think it should. In particular we cannot complain to God if a proverb 'fails'. God will always keep his promises, but he is under no obligation to ensure that a proverb is fulfilled.

Because there are always exceptions to proverbial statements, it is important not to use them to define doctrine. Nor are proverbs intended to be rules and regulations. A proverb is not in itself a command, but it can expand upon a command and back it up. For instance, a proverb might tell you what 'do not steal' means in practice, and illustrate why such a command is important in real life.

As such, proverbs do moralise. The ancient sages believed that an inherent morality was fundamental to the created order, both to the natural world and to men. Proverbial wisdom enables men to live in harmony with this universal order and guides them into appropriate behaviour for right living. Those who ignore this wisdom, and go their own way regardless of this advice, are thus called foolish.

We also learn something from the English word 'proverb' itself. This is made up of two parts: 'pro' and 'verb' where 'pro' means 'for' and 'verb' is short for 'verbum', which means 'word'. So a pro-verb is a 'word for' a particular occasion or situation. This highlights that a proverb is not a universal truth or may not always be what is required. Rather it aims to be the right word at the right time.

It also explains why proverbs can contradict each other. We find this in English proverbs. Will many hands make the work easier, or will more cooks only get in each other's way? Both can be true in their own way at certain times, according to situations and circumstances. Should I look before leaping or will such hesitation lead to loss? Perhaps this depends if you are intending to get married or wanting to grab a bargain in a sale.

Part of being wise is being able to discern when a particular proverb is the right one. Which one applies when? Knowing that they are just general observations on life should mean we realise they provide some advice but not necessarily the final answer. Rather they are intended to stir our little grey cells into action!

We also find contradictory proverbs in the book of Proverbs, in one case right next to each other in consecutive verses. In Proverbs 26:4-5 we read: 'Do not answer a fool according to his folly, or you yourself will be just like him.' This is followed straightaway with: 'Answer a fool according to his folly, or he will be wise in his own eyes.'

Here are two clashing proverbs side by side. So do we answer or not? Is it a wise move to engage in conversation with fools? This may depend upon the person involved and what kind of folly they are uttering. We should also assess how they might react. In some situations it may not be worth the argument. If it makes you look equally foolish, then better to keep quiet. At other times it may be beneficial. If you can make it obvious what is being said is nothing more than foolishness, then you may prevent someone from thinking they are wise when they clearly aren't. So do we answer or not? As a wise man once said, there is 'a time to be silent and a time to speak' (Eccles. 3:7b). Over to you to decide!

In summary, the aim of a proverb is to comment on the underlying patterns of life by summarising a multitude of observations into simple generalities and tendencies. The task of the proverb compiler is to search out analogies and comparisons, present them for our consideration, and then leave us to make our own decision.

Proverbs both teach wisdom and also require wisdom if they are to be used correctly. They are not magic formulae. They do not bring wisdom through simple incantation. Repeat a proverb often enough and lo and behold, a result! In fact, a misused proverb can cause pain and harm, as Proverbs 26:9 makes clear: 'Like a thorn-bush in a drunkard's hand is a proverb in the mouth of a fool.' We cannot just fling proverbs around in the hope that wisdom will be the outcome.

Proverbs are very successful at being proverbs, being what they are designed to be, delivering wisdom within their accepted limitations. They offer some rationale for our decision making. But if we regard them as being prophetic or providing a systematic theology, then they will fail us, and we will end up more confused or frustrated.

What can be frustrating about proverbs is that they seem to make life appear a bit too neat and tidy. Because they generalise, they make sweeping statements. Choosing wisdom leads to prosperity and life; choosing folly brings ruin and death. It is this black-and-white over-optimistic approach to life which raises most questions and leads to the protesting arguments we find elsewhere in the wisdom books. Of course, we cannot really find fault with proverbs if they are simply obeying their own nature. It is what they are like and cannot be otherwise. Nevertheless, the accusation that proverbs are over-simplistic is one we will have to address in due course.

Meanwhile, in our next chapter we will examine one proverb in detail, as a sort of case study. How well have we understood that very well-known proverb in 22:6 about starting children off on the way they should go?

Chapter Eight

Proverbs 22:6, A Case Study

In this chapter we will aim for a better insight into the well-known proverb about a child's upbringing found in Proverbs 22:6. Part of the issue involves how it is usually translated, so before we tackle this particular saying in detail we will touch on some of the difficulties encountered when translating proverbs from Hebrew into English.

One such issue is due to the brevity of Hebrew proverbs, and indeed of proverbs generally. We saw in the last chapter that a biblical proverb aims to make its point as briefly as possible. It's the same in English. Do you prefer, 'In advance of committing yourself to a course of action consider carefully all your various options', or the more succinct, 'Look before you leap'? Or what about, 'If you take certain corrective measures early enough in the course of action you will forestall major problems from arising later'? Isn't 'A stitch in time saves nine' much better?

Translating these from English could prove challenging. It may need more than four words in the former case, and struggle to keep the alliteration of 'look' and leap'. When it comes to the English saying about sewing, 'nine' is chosen to form an assonance with 'time'. There is nothing special about that number otherwise. Your early stitch might save eight, ten or twenty-three, but nine is better in English. So what would this number become in translation?

Overall, we can see why each language creates its own proverbs rather than attempts to translate those from elsewhere. But unless we learn to read Hebrew we do need an English version of the book of Proverbs. And this causes a particular issue as Hebrew proverbs are usually only seven or eight words long, and that is the whole couplet. English translations tend to have to increase this number, often to twice as many. Moreover, our translation may add words that aren't there to make it a more normal English sentence.

For instance, a Hebrew proverb can make its point without using verbs, simply by juxtaposing terms within the parallelism. Proverbs 10:5 literally reads, 'A gatherer in summer, a wise son, a sleeper during harvest, a disgraceful son.' That's just eight Hebrew words. You won't find anything that concise in English. For instance, the NIV has, 'He who gathers crops in summer is a prudent son, but he who sleeps during harvest is a disgraceful son.' That's twenty words. In the next verse (10:6), there are just seven Hebrew words compared to the English fifteen or sixteen. It is impossible to match the brevity completely.

But more significant is the way this can affect how we understand a proverb. In the first part of 12:1 we have just four Hebrew words, basically, 'Loving discipline, loving knowledge.' An English translation tends to include the word 'whoever', so we get, 'Whoever loves discipline, loves knowledge.' Here the comparison is stressed by forming a subject-predicate sentence. Here comes the technical bit! A subject-predicate sentence is one which has a particular subject and which makes a statement about it. In this example, the subject is someone who loves discipline and the consequence is that he will love knowledge also. But the Hebrew is more ambiguous. It simply puts two things side by side rather than make a statement about one in terms of the other. So in Hebrew it can also mean, 'Whoever loves knowledge, loves discipline.' The Hebrew text allows it to work either way round, whereas the English translation has made a particular choice and so removed the possible interpretation of it being the other way round. Does this matter too much? Probably not. But it does illustrate the difference between the original and a translation.

Another example is in 17:19, where there are just eight Hebrew words which basically say, 'Loving sin, loving strife, making high his gate, seeking destruction.' In English, we find the word 'whoever' is usually inserted twice, creating two separate clauses and so reducing the range of interpretation. In fact, the NIV has swapped the first two around, 'Whoever loves a quarrel loves sin.' This may be true, but isn't 'Whoever loves sin loves a quarrel' equally valid?

In chapter 25 we find further examples of simple juxtapositions in Hebrew to which the English version has added extra explanatory words. In verse 3 we have, 'The sky for height, the earth for depth, the heart of kings is unsearchable' (25:3). The English version starts off with 'As' and later adds 'so'. Hence we have, 'As the heavens are high and the earth is deep, so the hearts of kings are unsearchable.' This is done in order to stress that the first two phrases are coupled together to provide a double comparison with the third. In this case, we could argue that this provides a helpful clarification.

A second example is in 25:25, where the Hebrew reads, 'Cold waters to a thirsty soul, good news from a far country.' In English this is spelt out a bit more: 'Like cold water to a thirsty soul, is good news from a distant land.' Again, this is hardly a real issue. But in some cases how a proverb is translated does affect what we think it means. To this end, we will spend the rest of this chapter examining in detail that very well-known proverb about bringing up a child.

In the NIV, Proverbs 22:6 reads, 'Start children off on the way they should go, and even when they are old they will not turn from it.' Twenty-one words in English when there are only eight in Hebrew!

The NKJV is equally verbose but opens slightly differently, 'Train up a child in the way he should go, and when he is old he will not depart from it.' This might be more familiar to long-standing Bible readers. But what do we make of this verse?

From what we have said before, we know we cannot claim this as a promise. There is no guarantee that even if a parent brings up a child correctly then all will be well for the rest of their life. This at least means parents need not feel guilty or a failure if after all their efforts their child remains wayward. Perhaps we should just be content with knowing that the proverb will generally be true, continue to be a good parent and hope for the best. But ultimately this seems a rather unsatisfactory, even negative, way of reading the proverb. Perhaps there is something better we can get from it?

For some, this proverb advocates what has been called the adaptive training approach to child rearing. This says it is the duty of every parent to observe carefully their God-given child and discover their innate abilities and characteristics. Parents are then to encourage their child along that path all the way to maturity. Finding, clarifying and reinforcing these qualities and abilities, will help the child find 'the way he should go'. This is preferable for a child rather than being forced to go the way their parents insist on. Being 'a chip off the old block' or 'following in their father's footsteps' may work for some but should not be imposed.

This explanation of the proverb seems reasonable, commendable even. It's certainly not a bad approach to child rearing but it lacks the moral dimension expected from a proverb. Moreover, this adaptive view is very modern and western. It is not part of the ancient world, or particularly Hebraic in any way. It is also inadequate in terms of the actual words of the proverb. So let's investigate these eight Hebrew words and see if a better understanding emerges.

The first Hebrew word in Proverbs 22:6 is *chanoch*, from the root h-n-k, which also forms the basis of the word Hanukkah, which is known to mean dedication through the Feast of Hanukkah, which celebrated the rededication of the Temple in Jerusalem in the second century BC. So already we see that 'train up' is not a good way to begin the verse. 'Dedicate' would be fine, as would 'start, initiate or inaugurate'.

We learn more about this word *chanoch* from its other appearances in the Old Testament. There are only four such instances and they all relate to a building not a person. The first use is in Deuteronomy 20:5, where it appears twice and refers to a newly built house yet to be lived in. The context is that someone who has just built a house and is yet to live in it, is exempt from going to war in case he dies and someone else gets to live in it. The repeated phrase 'live in it' is actually 'dedicate it'. This does not imply a special ceremony or celebration. It simply means the initial occasion of something that would continue. The same idea is also behind the use of this word for the dedication of Solomon's Temple in 1 Kings 8:63 and 2 Chronicles 7:5. This is when it started to function in God's service in the way it was meant to.

So when in Proverbs 22:6 this word refers to a child, it is suggesting this is about something that will happen from the very beginning of his or her life. We shall see shortly what this 'something' is.

As for the word 'child', this is *na'ar*, which is used around 250 times in the Old Testament in a variety of ways, with a wide age span from infant to thirty years old. It commonly means a youth, but in our case a young child is fine, a child from their earliest days onwards.

The next word is a strange one, *al-pi*. This is an idiom and is literally 'upon the mouth of'. It is used to mean 'after the measure of', or 'according to the standard of'. It can be reduced to the simpler 'according to', which makes sense in any English translation.

So far, then, in Proverbs 22:6 we have, 'Initiate a child on the mouth of his way' or, 'Initiate a child according to his way'. But we have now reached the crucial part of the verse. What is this 'way', and in particular is it one in which, as English translations suggest, 'he should go'?

The Hebrew word for 'way' is *darko*, from the root d-r-k, which also gives us *derek* meaning 'path' or 'way'. The suffix '-o' tells us it is the third person masculine, so 'his way' is an accurate translation. Whenever this word *darko* occurs in Proverbs it always means the way that a person has chosen for himself unless there is another word nearby (called a qualifier), which adjusts the meaning and takes it away from its natural sense. In Proverbs 22:6 there is no qualifier in Hebrew; it is literally 'his own way' and should remain as such in translation. But English versions insist upon modifying it somehow, usually by 'the way *he should go*'. This creates the impression that this 'way' is something moral or religious, suggesting the child should be trained in 'the right way' or 'in God's way'. This may seem plausible but it is not what the text is saying. To understand it like this requires making changes which the words do not allow for.

In addition, a proverb is an isolated saying contained totally within a single verse, so we cannot look for the meaning of 'his way' in the preceding or following verse; 'his' has to refer back to the child himself mentioned earlier in the proverb. Incidentally, the phrase 'God's way' is not typical Hebrew thinking. Rather, it would use the word 'walk'; the way 'he should walk' would tell us this is about parents bringing up their child to follow God and his commands.

So we have to conclude this proverb is telling us something about the way that a child chooses for himself. But letting a child have his own way is usually a recipe for disaster, and seems to contradict everything else that Proverbs teaches about instructing a child in the words of the wise. Where does that leave us?

Our dilemma is resolved once we realise this verse is not issuing a command but a warning. It is not an instruction on how to bring up a child, but a warning that if you allow a child to go his own way from the start then he won't deviate from it later in life; he will turn out badly. Again, like all proverbs, this is a generalisation, but a valid one based upon observation.

Technically this is still a command but one which is known as an ironic imperative. Irony is when a speaker intends to convey a sense contrary to the strict meaning of the words used. The aim is not to produce the action commanded, rather the very opposite. We occasionally speak like this. 'You do that!' can mean 'Don't you dare do that' or 'You do that and you'll see what happens!' This type of speech occurs in the Bible. Jesus himself in John 2:19 said, 'Destroy this temple', meaning his body. But he wasn't telling them to kill him. Rather, if you do this, then I'll be raised anyway. Go ahead, and see what happens next!

We should continue to look at the Hebrew words in Proverbs 22:6 to check this understanding remains valid. The rest reads, 'Even should he grow old, he will not turn from it'. 'Even' is better than 'and' (used in most translations) as it is not a given that he will grow old. But, we are warned, even if he does live a long life then we can expect him to continue in the same way in which he has been allowed to start life.

'He will not turn from it' is usually seen as meaning he will not forsake his godly upbringing. However, the word 'turn' (*soor*) can mean either to turn from good to evil or from evil to good. In Proverbs, most of the time (thirteen out of seventeen) it refers to turning from evil to good. So the final part of the proverb is saying that even if a child does reach maturity, then he will not naturally turn away from the start that indulgent or wayward parents have allowed. It can seem easier for a parent to let a child do his own thing, go his own way. Much less effort is involved than in enforcing discipline all the time. But let a child think there are no borders to behaviour and that they can follow their own desires and impulses, then you have set in motion patterns that will be hard to change and which will dictate his life for the rest of his days. Do you really want this?

So overall, we can paraphrase the proverb as: 'Allow a child to start out according to the standards of his own choosing then even if he manages to grow old, he will not turn away from the evil of that way.' The Hebrew proverb says all this in just eight words!

Some of this chapter has perhaps been a bit technical at times but it is important to get at the real meaning of such texts. Next, we will return to the remaining collections in the book of Proverbs.

Chapter Nine

Proverbs:
Thirty Sayings of the Wise

In our study of the book of Proverbs, we have now reached a rather distinctive collection of proverbs called 'sayings of the wise'.

This section from 22:17 to 24:22 comes between the two Solomon collections and in some Bibles is set out specifically as Saying 1, Saying 2 and so on, under the general heading of 'Thirty Sayings of the Wise'. Back in chapter 6 we commented how scholars generally agree that this portion of Proverbs resembles in many ways an ancient Egyptian wisdom document from around 1200 BC entitled 'The Instruction of Amenemope' (or Amenemopet). This is also in thirty sections, each called 'a saying'. We also discussed how wisdom traditions flourished in ancient Egypt and elsewhere outside of Israel, and that it is quite understandable how some of this came to be included within the Hebrew Scriptures. We won't repeat all this here, so you may find it helpful to go back and refresh your memory before continuing with the rest of this chapter.

This section opens with a short passage in 22:17-21 which serves both to indicate a clear change from what has gone before as well as to introduce what is to follow. Here we find something similar to the opening prologue of the book of Proverbs generally. It sets the tone by exhorting us to pay attention and listen carefully. This is back to preaching rather than just presenting another set of observations. In particular, we are told to apply our heart to what is taught (v17). The instructions coming up should find a place deep within us and also be readily available on our lips to pass on to others (v18).

The opening verse also informs us that these proverbs are to be generally regarded as 'sayings of the wise', rather than specifically from Solomon. This allows for the possibility that they have been gathered from foreign sources then written down for the benefit of others. Or rather *rewritten*, for although there is evidence of the influence of the Egyptian material mentioned above, it is not merely a matter of copying. There are also signs of editing, either a simple adaptation or a more thorough reworking. This includes some slight differences in emphasis or a re-ordering of the sayings.

Experts who have studied the relationship between this section of Proverbs and 'The Instruction of Amenemope' say that the greatest similarities occur in the first eleven sayings, which takes us to 23:11. This includes the introductory verses which count as Saying 1. When we get to 23:12 (Saying 12) we find another exhortation to listen and apply instruction, perhaps marking the start of a new series. From this point, verbal similarities with Amenemope are less obvious, we are told, and what follows is more likely to be Israelite in origin.

While we can leave such detailed analysis to the experts there are some general points that are worth knowing. For instance, there are several themes in common with the Egyptian material, such as attitudes towards riches and the poor, and the issue of boundary stones. Also, this section is addressed to us more personally and directly. For instance, 'I teach you today, even you' (22:19). This increases the urgency of the sayings. As for further differences, there is more clustering than before, with some small units emerging quite distinctly, making this section more continuous than is the case with the Solomon collections. In addition, scholars also report that the metaphors and poetic reflections in these verses are more elegant than before. One final point of note is found in verse 19 where it states the purpose of learning these sayings is 'so that your trust may be in the LORD'. This specific desire to promote trust in Yahweh is one possible sign of editing to make this section more appropriate for inclusion in the Hebrew Bible.

As we look through the rest of this passage, we will not be providing a full commentary, more a case of edited highlights. We will pick out some of the details which will help us understand certain sayings better, so do have your Bible open at these chapters to help you as we go along.

We will start with the second saying in 22:22-23. This is in line with a general concern for the poor and needy as shown within the Torah. The words 'exploit' and 'crush' in verse 22 are particularly strong and chosen to reflect the seriousness of such actions. The phrase 'in court' refers to the city gate where justice was administered. If they are mistreated there, then ultimately the Lord will take up their case.

Saying 3, in verses 24-25, highlights the importance of choosing our friends carefully. We are more readily influenced by those we are closest to, and ultimately we become more like them than others.

In 22:26-27 (Saying 4) we find a warning against rash promises and foolish pledges, something which occurs earlier in Proverbs 6:1, 11:15 and 17:18. In these we find that making a deal by shaking hands is also mentioned. In those days a bed was a luxury enjoyed by few. Most slept on the floor with their cloak as their only covering. To lose your bed would be a serious loss but, equally, pledging your cloak could be risky. That's why there are commands in the Torah to return it by sunset (see Exod. 22:26, Deut. 24:10-13).

Saying 5 (22:28) and Saying 11 (23:10-11) both refer to ancient boundary stones. These were property markers going back to the initial conquest of the land and its division. As such they were a recognition of family inheritances, giving rights that were not to be tampered with (see Deut. 19:14). Moving them to gain more land for yourself was theft. In Proverbs 23:11 we find mention of a defender or redeemer. In some translations this may be capitalised, suggesting that this is God. Although God certainly does take a special interest in the fatherless, this verse may be referring to the kinsman-redeemer whose duty it was to look after the property interests of those who were orphans or without close relatives (see Lev. 25:25).

Moving into chapter 23, the first three verses give advice on what to do when invited to dine in exalted company. The first verse contains an ambiguity. It either refers to the meal itself (*what* is before you) or to your dinner companions (*who* are before you). In reality, there is little difference in meaning. Both could be true. Don't complain about the food or your fellow guests. Behaving well and being complimentary in all circumstances can only be for your good.

The comment in verse 2 about putting a knife to your throat is not, of course, to be taken literally. Rather it is a health warning to curb your appetite when faced with a sumptuous feast. Gluttony is not only a sin, but excessive eating of such delicacies may endanger your life. In addition, overeating displays a poor attitude at such a feast.

The word 'deceptive' in verse 3 is also ambiguous. It may be another health warning. Such delicacies themselves may be deceptive. They look good but may be less nourishing and lead to bad health. Or it could refer to the sly nature of the host who is plying his guest with such goodies. What does he want in return?

Saying 8 (23:4-5) is not claiming that wealth is evil, rather that it is transitory and making its acquisition your goal can reduce the quality of life. Let wisdom guide you into how much money you should have. The wonderful imagery of money sprouting wings and flying out of your pocket is common in ancient wisdom. Easy come, easy go!

Proverbs 23:6-8 (Saying 9) returns to the theme of dining with someone who, in this case, turns out to be a stingy host. The phrase for 'stingy' in verse 6 is literally 'a bad eye', a common Hebraic idiom also used by Jesus, for instance in Matthew 6:22-23. Having a good eye means you are generous; a bad eye refers to meanness. (For more on this idiom see my book *Listening to the Jewish Jesus*.) Meanwhile, back in Proverbs chapter 23, part of verse 7 is rather obscure and difficult to translate with any certainty.

Referring to the host, it basically seems to be saying there is no enjoyment and little lasting value in sharing a meal with someone who is hypocritical, inhospitable and mean.

As we said earlier, 23:12 is a general exhortation serving to introduce the sayings that follow. The first of these, in verses 13-14, is also part of Egyptian wisdom as well as being remarkably similar to an Assyrian saying from the seventh century BC. Corporal punishment was accepted throughout the ancient world and seen as beneficial. It won't kill you but it might save you from premature physical death.

Saying 15, 23:17-18, is similar to 24:19-20 (Saying 29). Both of these concern our inner feelings whenever we see wicked people seemingly having a better time than us. It is easy to envy them or become fretful. How do they get away with wrongdoing? This is a common problem, also discussed in some of the wisdom psalms, which we will study in a later chapter, but for now it is worth quoting the opening of Psalm 37: 'Do not fret because of those who are evil or be envious of those who do wrong; for like the grass they will soon wither, like green plants they will soon die away' (Ps. 37:1-2). The way to counter these feelings of envy is to take the long view. Think about their future. They have no hope. At this stage in Israel's history there was no detailed understanding of an afterlife involving rewards and punishment but it was generally agreed that being zealous for the Lord and fearing him was the best option.

Saying 19 brings chapter 23 to a conclusion. In verses 29-35, the longest and most evocative of all the Sayings, we are treated to a vivid picture of the plight of a drunkard. Full of insight, drama and pathos, this is one of the most memorable passages in the whole of Proverbs. Two opening questions draw us into the scene: literally it says, 'Who has "Oh"? Who has "Alas"?' Four more questions follow, where strife refers to physical scuffles and struggles, and complaints are the verbal arguments drunkenness can lead to. The wounds without cause, or needless bruises, are either self-inflicted through intoxication or the result of conflicts that would be avoidable if not in a drunken state. The answer to all these questions is in the next verse, verse 30, namely those who drink excessively and habitually. They linger over their wine, staying up late to sample all that is available.

Then comes a graphic description of the wine itself. It is enticing and strong, well fermented. It sparkles, catching the eye in an appealing fashion. Its allure can only be resisted by not gazing into the cup. Verse 32 onwards relates the outcome of too much wine. The after-effects are like a poisonous snake bite, including hallucinations, lack of rational thought and speech, and a sensation of instability similar to being on a storm-tossed sea. In verse 34 the word 'rigging' means the top of something. This may refer to the top of a ship (not the best place to be in a storm), but is better thought of as the crest of the waves, the top of the sea as it churns in a storm. It is interesting that Psalm 107:25-27 uses the same image in reverse. The plight of sailors in a fierce storm is compared to that of drunkards staggering about! This expressive depiction of a drunkard ends sadly. He is at the mercy of those who treat him badly, and as soon as he recovers from his hangover he starts to look for his next drink. It's a life of addiction accompanied by a continual sense of desperation.

Proverbs 24:10 can stand on its own but also forms part of a longer saying with the next two verses. Verse 10 is phrased as a conditional statement (if you falter) but is also an accusation. You falter and all will know how weak you are! There is also wordplay here between trouble = pressure and small = depressed or squeezed. In itself, verse 11 is unclear. Are those being led away to death innocent victims or being rightly punished? The former seems better as this links back to the faltering courage and strength in verse 10. Failing to rescue or help by intervening in some way is unacceptable. Standing by and doing nothing has no defence. Claims we did not know what was going on or that we really couldn't do anything, are just excuses, and God knows it!

The final saying (24:21-22) also has translational issues. The second half of verse 21 can read either 'do not disobey either of them' (the king or God) or 'do not associate with those who change', which is translated as the rebellious, meaning those who seek change by challenging the authority of God and the king. In verse 22, the words 'those two' clearly refer to both God and the king. We are to realise that just as rebellion against the supreme ruler in the land brings retribution, so also does defiance of the supreme ruler of heaven and earth. The wrath of an earthly king acts as a good illustration of that of the heavenly king.

Our brief survey of these nuggets of wisdom should be enough to convince us that, whatever their origin, they can be applied to all people everywhere. It is ultimately irrelevant whether or not they were Egyptian imports into the Jewish tradition; they belong to us all now.

As for the rest of chapter 24, this is another shorter collection which has been added onto the previous Thirty Sayings. Their authorship or origin is not mentioned but the opening (v23) indicates these are also to be considered as 'sayings of the wise'. One point of interest is that two of these verses, 33 and 34, are identical to an earlier pairing in 6:10-11. Quite why is not clear but they each seem to act as a conclusion to their respective sections, 6:6-11 and 24:30-34.

In our next chapter we will turn to the second Solomon collection, found in chapters 25 to 29.

Chapter Ten

Proverbs: Chapters 25 to 29

We are now approaching the end of the book of Proverbs and have reached the section generally known as the second collection of Solomon which occupies chapters 25 to 29.

We have already said something about this collection in chapter 6, in particular that it opens with 'These are more proverbs of Solomon' and then continues with 'compiled by the men of Hezekiah king of Judah'. We commented then how this demonstrates that Proverbs is a composite work put together over a long period of time. Even if the first collection of Solomon was produced during or just after his reign (ca. 970 to 930 BC) then this collection must have been put together well over 200 years later, during the reign of Hezekiah (ca. 716 to 687 BC). Indeed there is no guarantee that this completed the whole process. The final version of what we now know as the book of Proverbs might not have been settled until much later.

One interesting question is why this second collection was placed at this point within the book of Proverbs rather than added onto the end of his first collection. Was this a deliberate choice by Hezekiah's men or perhaps by a later editor? Or does it reflect the randomness and lack of overall plan of the book as a whole? Certainly it would not be natural to place it at the very end of the book, after the three remaining sections in chapters 30 and 31.

Another intriguing question is what is meant in the opening verse by 'compiled'. Some translations opt instead for 'copied'. Greek versions in particular use the word *exegrapsanto*, meaning 'to write something out for yourself'. It is quite feasible that Hezekiah's men did copy out these sayings rather than just gather them, as they were probably officials in the royal court who would be skilled as scribes.

However, the Hebrew word in 25:1 is *hetiqu*, which comes from a root meaning 'to move', often used for moving something around. In what sense did Hezekiah's men 'move these sayings around'? Could this mean they transcribed them or organised them in some way? Or does it refer to a physical transposition, an actual change in location? Perhaps they were found in one place and then moved to another, to sit alongside other proverbs as part of this larger book.

Part of the issue is that we don't know how Hezekiah's men obtained these sayings in the first place. Did they suddenly discover them, or were they already well known and in common use? Perhaps Solomon hadn't recorded them in his lifetime. Instead they had been passed on orally and remembered that way. Maybe now it was decided that this was the time to write them out and gather them alongside others, and this was the task that Hezekiah's men undertook.

We have discussed previously how the phrase 'proverbs of Solomon' does not necessarily mean they were originally written or produced by him. He may have collected them from elsewhere. However, the consensus is that such proverbs are most likely the work of Solomon himself. Certainly with this collection, neither Hezekiah nor his officials claim authorship for themselves. They offer them to us as 'more proverbs of Solomon'. Most scholars agree these proverbs do come from the time of Solomon, though some later editorial work on them was probably undertaken. Overall, we can accept they did originate with Solomon, with Hezekiah's men providing some editing and arranging, 'moving them about' in some way to bring them together and place them alongside other collections.

Finally, if these sayings were not already known and in use, how did they suddenly reappear after so long? One option is that they were discovered in the Temple when Hezekiah had it cleaned out as part of his reforms (2 Chr. 29). If so, then no doubt the proverbs would be readily received as part of Israel's religious restoration, a welcome reminder of what their faith once was and should be like again.

The opening verse of chapter 25 may provide some uncertainty regarding these sayings but after that we are back on familiar ground. In chapters 25 to 29 we find the same keen observation of life as before, with the same style and mix of parallel types, synonymous and antithetic. There is still no obvious structure but one topic that prevails in these chapters is that of kingship or of being a ruler generally. We find occasional mentions of kings and royalty in earlier collections, but now this theme is more apparent. This begins in 25:2, which is quite well-known. 'It is the glory of God to conceal a matter; to search out a matter is the glory of kings.' Overall, such proverbs urge the people to look up to a king as God's representative, but equally the king must look to God for the source of his own authority, and make it a priority to bring God's justice and righteousness to the people.

Another familiar saying from this collection is found in 27:17, where the phrase 'as iron sharpens iron' occurs. People often quote this without realising where it comes from! And there are several other proverbs in these chapters which should also ring a bell.

Proverbs 25:6-7 exhorts us not to exalt ourselves in the king's presence as we may find later that we are humbled before others. Rather we are to wait for the king to say, 'Come up here.' This is remarkably similar to Jesus' parable in Luke 14:7-11 of a wedding feast, where taking the highest place of honour might equally result in humiliation if we are told to give it up to someone more important. Jesus teaches us to start at the lowest place and wait to be called up higher.

Another example is in Proverbs 26:11, which reads, 'As a dog returns to its vomit, so fools repeat their folly.' The opening words of this proverb are directly quoted in 2 Peter 2:22.

Then there is Proverbs 27:1, 'Do not boast about tomorrow, for you do not know what a day may bring.' This is expanded upon by James in 4:13-17 of his letter.

Meanwhile, in Romans 12:20 there is another direct quote from this portion of Proverbs, this time from 25:21-22. 'If your enemy is hungry feed him; if he is thirsty, give him something to drink. In doing this, you will heap burning coals on his head.' What a strange idea! Treat your enemy well, then seriously hurt or injure him! The context in Romans is about not taking revenge, but leaving this to the Lord. Rather we are to overcome evil with good. How do hot coals on the head achieve this? Here, it seems, is an isolated text being used in an erroneous manner, until, that is, we realise this is a proverb and so may be invoking an idiomatic expression or poetic image we are not familiar with. Most likely, to heap burning coals on someone's head is to cause them to repent, which is the outcome hoped for by offering your enemy food and drink. The imagery is that of a sacrifice being made in order to express sorrow or repentance, perhaps a burnt offering which would require such coals. The more precise picture is of someone going to the Temple to make such an offering, carrying his burning coals on a tray on his head. This still seems painful, and may not be that literal, which is where the idiomatic or illustrative nature of a proverb comes into play.

From these examples we can see how New Testament writers drew inspiration from Proverbs. We should also remember that Jesus grew up with this book. It was part of his education, and it is not surprising that Jesus echoes such earlier wisdom as part of his own teaching.

There are many more examples of how proverbs are used in the New Testament. Why not find some for yourself? Here are two more to get you started. See how Proverbs

3:34 is quoted in James 4:6 and 1 Peter 5:5, and also how James 5:20 and 1 Peter 4:8 draw upon Proverbs 10:12.

Next, we will turn to chapter 30 and the sayings of Agur. Who exactly was he, and what contribution did he make to this book?

Chapter Eleven

Proverbs: Chapter 30, The Sayings of Agur

In our study of the book of Proverbs we have now reached the penultimate chapter, chapter 30, which consists of the sayings of Agur. Here we shall be trying to determine who he was and what contribution his sayings make to the book of Proverbs.

Let's start with the person of Agur himself. Identifying exactly who Agur was can be quite tricky, despite there being some clues. He is described as the son of Jakeh but that doesn't get us much further forward. These names are not of Hebrew origin, so it is readily assumed that Agur is a non-Israelite. But did he convert to Judaism or is he another one of those wise men from elsewhere who have contributed some worthwhile 'sayings of the wise' (22:17)?

Agur is generally regarded as being an Ishmaelite and that he lived in a region of northern Arabia called Massa. But here, right at the start in verse 1, we meet our first ambiguity and issue regarding translation. After his name and that of his father comes the Hebrew word *hamasa*, which has two possible meanings. One is that Agur is a

Massa-ite, someone descended from the tribe of Massa. Massa was the seventh of the twelve sons of Ishmael mentioned in Genesis 25:14. These sons became tribal rulers and settled near the eastern border with Egypt, towards Ashur (see Gen. 25:13-18), though it may be that some migrated into northern Arabia later. Historians report that the kingdom of Massa is mentioned in certain Assyrian and early north Arabian inscriptions, locating it about 250 miles south-east of Aqaba, which makes it one of the desert tribes of north-western Arabia.

We shall meet this same translational issue again at the start of chapter 31 regarding King Lemuel, where we find the related Hebrew word *masa*. (Note that *ha-* at the front of a Hebrew word just indicates it is preceded by the word 'the', so *masa* and *hamasa* are basically the same noun.) If 31:1 means that Lemuel was also of the tribe of Massa then he may have been Agur's king. Maybe Agur served in his court, as one of his officials or wise men. But this is all speculation; they may not even have been contemporaries.

Moreover we said that *hamasa* can have another meaning. Rather than the letters being transliterated into Massa, the name of a person or place, it can be translated into something like 'oracle' or 'inspired utterance'. Many English versions favour this, both in 30:1 and in 31:1 regarding Lemuel. But an oracle is usually a prophetic statement not a proverbial one, and carries with it the sense of being a burden, another word sometimes used in translating Proverbs 30:1. The word 'portentous' is also often attached to such an utterance. Here is an ominous warning! So if *hamasa* is to be translated as such, and not taken as referring to Massa, then this would make Agur's sayings of a different kind to those of Solomon, or indeed of any elsewhere in Proverbs. We have to ask, do these sayings of Agur really act in a prophetic way or as portents of doom?

The full phrase in 30:1 is *hamasa ne'um* where the second word provides the sense of something being uttered. We find this word elsewhere, for instance regarding David's last words in 2 Samuel 23:1 which are also described as an inspired utterance, and also with respect to Balaam's prophecies in Numbers 24:3, 15. The same idea is also contained in the phrase the 'oracle of Yahweh', sometimes just translated as 'declares the LORD', for instance in Jeremiah 23:4, 11, 12. In each case what is being said is regarded as prophetic not proverbial. We could perhaps accept the word 'inspired' to reflect the nature of Agur's sayings, rather than prophetic in the way we usually think.

It is noticeable that the NIV renders this part of verse 1 as: 'an inspired utterance. This man's utterance to . . .' Why the repetition of 'utterance'? If *hamasa* is not about Massa, the place or person, but is translated as 'oracle' or 'utterance', then it makes sense to split the phrase *hamasa ne'um* and attach *ne'um* to the following word *hageber,* the man. Hence, we get a new sentence beginning 'This man's utterance'. However, if *hamasa* is referring to Massa, then we can simply have 'The sayings of Agur, son of Jakeh, from Massa, an (inspired) utterance to . . .'

So perhaps after all this it is best to say that Agur was a famous sage of Massa, capable of producing the sort of proverbs that were thought worthy of being included in this book. But the dilemma remains. Moreover, our difficulties have only just begun! And we are not yet at the end of verse 1! Here is an inspired utterance to . . . whom?

The rest of verse 1 in Hebrew reads *le'eetiel le'eetiel ve-ucal*. You don't need to be a Hebrew expert to notice the repetition. So what's going on here? As before, these words can be transliterated into proper names, Ithiel and Ucal, or translated into other words. If they are names then what we have here is 'This man's utterance to Ithiel, to Ithiel and Ucal', which is a rather unusual way of making such an address, though perhaps more acceptable within a poetic context.

So the other option is not to take them as names but as verbs or verbal clauses, which leads to the tricky problem of how to translate them as such, and also what to make of the initial repetition. One solution to the issue of repetition is to regard Ithiel as being a name in the first instance, but not in the second. Otherwise, what you choose for a translation of *le'eetiel* also has to be repeated.

One typical translation for *le'eetiel* is 'I am weary, O God'. Note the ending *–el* which gives us 'God' or 'O God'. The second word, *ucal*, also presents options, so the phrase is variously completed as 'I am weary, O God, and faint, exhausted, spent, consumed or without power'. Any of these would lead well into the next verse, so something of this kind is now the view of most translators and commentators. However, some prefer to render *ucal* as 'prevailed' or 'triumphed'. Basically, I'm all done in but have come out a winner!

But then again, some translators take *le'eetiel* to mean something entirely different, either 'I am not God' or 'There is no God', which totally changes the way we should understand Agur and his role in Proverbs. These translations then come out as, 'There is no God and I cannot know anything' or 'I am not God that I should have power.' For some, yet another option would be, 'I have struggled with God and triumphed.' But that leaves us wondering what kind of struggle he engaged in, and in what way he triumphed. A struggle against God perhaps, or against conventional wisdom?

We will have to leave it to the experts in Hebrew to judge the merits of these various translations but we can see how troublesome this verse is and how it creates doubt on who Agur is and what he is saying. Is he a sceptic, an agnostic, a total non-believer? In which case, what about verse 5 where he appears to believe everything God says and verse 7 where he addresses the Lord in faith?

To solve this issue, some scholars say that only verses 1 to 3, or at most verses 1 to 4, are actually by Agur, which means he is definitely a sceptic of some kind. Then in what follows, in verses 5 to 6, we get a believer's response to his views. So overall, we are being presented with a dialogue, a juxtaposition of agnostic views with those of an orthodox believer. Effectively we are witnessing a dispute between opposing schools of wisdom: one orthodox, the other presenting a challenge to the prevailing views of the time. Under this scenario, the same challenge is being made to us. Where do we stand on this matter? Another option is that Agur is denying the existence of God or saying he has no knowledge of him, in order to be refuted. If so then what we have here is an example of a typical teaching method involving role play. Agur is acting a part to see how we respond.

In verses 2 and 3 we again have a choice on how to interpret Agur's words. He may be genuinely lamenting his lack of wisdom and displaying a humility that shows a true desire for divine knowledge. Or maybe he is still being sceptical, mocking those who think him brutish, like the animals, because he does not accept the traditional wisdom that comes from God. How we read these verses will probably depend on how we view this passage as a whole.

As for verse 4, it is noticeably much longer than other verses in the chapter, indeed than in Proverbs as a whole, and full of demanding rhetorical questions, five in total, all wrapped up in cynicism. It appears Agur is again mocking those who claim to have divine wisdom and who therefore know such things. He is prepared to question how much we really can know of God's ways.

These questions are reminiscent of those in Isaiah 40:12-14 and also in parts of Job chapters 38 and 39 where God questions Job (see Job 38:5, 8, 25, 36-37, 39:5). Is it possible Agur could have been aware of these and was attempting something similar to support his claim that attaining such knowledge is beyond us? Or was he just employing a general way of expressing such doubt? If Agur was trying to copy something known to him, then verse 5 is upholding the original questions as the word of God and warning Agur not to play around with them.

The use of 'Who' or 'Whose' in these questions is basically asking, 'Which man has done these things?' The answer to each, of course, is no-one. Only God can do these things. The last of these questions confirms that the questioner is thinking in human terms by asking, 'What is his name, and what is the name of his son?' This is not implying that God has a son. There is no sudden theological leap at this point. Rather this is a parallelism, similar to Psalm 8:4, 'What is man that you are mindful of him, the son of man that you care for him?'

From verse 7 onwards the chapter gets easier! Once more we are treated to some vivid observations. Agur is another keen onlooker on life who says exactly what he sees. One strong feature of his sayings is the use of so-called numerical proverbs which give the chapter its own special flavour. In particular he regularly uses the form x, x+1 where a number is followed by the next one (known as consecutive integers). For instance, the second half of verse 15 reads, 'There are three things that are never satisfied, four that never say, "Enough!"' Further examples can be found in verses 18, 21 and 29.

This format provides an in-built crescendo or sense of progression but without providing any numerical exactness. There is no precise figure intended here. Rather, when you think you have counted them all, there is still another one. Incidentally, this kind of saying has occurred once before, in Proverbs 6:16-19. There is also an example in Job 5:19, and many more in Amos chapters 1 and 2.

Two of the proverbs stand alone from the surrounding numerical sayings. One is verse 17 with its theme of disrespect for parents, common throughout Proverbs and mentioned earlier in this chapter in verse 11. Incidentally, vultures do not attack living people, only dead bodies, so the imagery here suggests a premature death for the offender, together with the disgrace of being denied a proper burial. The other is in verse 20 where the impact comes from the thought of an adulteress regarding her activities as no worse than enjoying a good meal. Self-deception is at the heart of her attitude towards what she does.

We cannot end without mentioning the wonderful imagery in verse 33 of churning cream, twisting noses and the stirring up of anger. There is also a neat piece of wordplay in that the word for 'nose' is the same as that for 'anger'. Just as pressure on the nose by twisting it draws blood, so the pressure of anger stirred up brings its own bloodshed.

Agur has provided a fresh voice to the book of Proverbs, especially the scepticism at the start of the chapter which stands against the usual simple, even superficial and sometimes over-optimistic view of proverbial wisdom. We shall meet more of this later when we study Job and Ecclesiastes. Meanwhile, we will next look through the final chapter of Proverbs, chapter 31, which contains some sayings of King Lemuel and a delightfully constructed poem extolling the virtues of a wife of noble character.

Chapter Twelve

Proverbs: Chapter 31, Sayings of King Lemuel and a Poem on the Wife of Noble Character

We have now reached the final chapter of the book of Proverbs which divides into two parts. In the first we have some more proverbial sayings, this time from King Lemuel. This is followed by a well-known poem on the ideal wife.

We start with the first nine verses where we find the 'sayings of King Lemuel', but who exactly was he? We mentioned in the last chapter the textual difficulty involved in deciding if Agur was from the tribe of Massa or whether the Hebrew word *hamasa* referred to his inspired utterance rather than his origin. We said then this issue would reappear in 31:1 regarding Lemuel, giving us the same two options. Some translations, probably most, interpret this as 'an inspired utterance' or 'prophecy', while others choose to refer to him as King Lemuel of Massa, which places him in northern Arabia.

The Hebrew text is clear that he was a king (*melech*) but this may simply indicate that he was a relatively minor ruler over a tribe or city, so it is not surprising if nothing much is known about him. His name, Lemuel, sounds like a Hebrew name with its –*el* ending. In which case it would mean one who is 'from God' or 'belonging to God' or even 'dedicated to God'. But it is possible for people with Hebrew names not to be Hebrew or Israelite. One suggestion is that Lemuel might have converted to Judaism. Then there is also the curious idea that this may be another way of describing Solomon himself, rather than the name of someone more obscure. The same theory has also been advanced regarding Agur, but in neither case is there a good reason for this. Overall, it is best to regard the proverbs in chapters 30 and 31 as non-Israelite in origin, more foreign 'sayings of the wise' (see 22:17).

Chapter 31 features two very different women: a concerned mother and an industrious wife. The sayings in verses 1-9 are reported as being taught to Lemuel by his mother. It doesn't say how old he was when this took place but the passage does read as though Lemuel was already king at the time. Incidentally, if Lemuel really was Solomon under another name, then Bathsheba would be the mother in question, a fact which may weigh against that particular theory.

However, it is not surprising that Lemuel received such maternal advice. Earlier in Proverbs we read twice that a son is not only to listen to his father's instruction but also not to forsake his mother's teaching (Prov. 1:8, 6:20). A mother had a vital role to play in passing on wisdom within the family. In general, mothers were looked upon with great esteem in the Ancient Near East, the mothers of kings especially so. They could have considerable influence in the royal court; some were given the title of queen mother (1 Kgs 2:19, 15:13).

Proverbs: Chapter 31,
Sayings of King Lemuel and a Poem on the Wife of Noble Character

As we have seen, the book of Proverbs opens with much fatherly advice to his son, so it is perhaps appropriate that it ends with a mother's counsel. In this case, being a royal mother, she addresses the responsibilities of a ruler, what is expected of him as a king. Her advice seems limited in scope but it is done with a personal touch. After all, this is not just any king, it is her actual son. The brevity of the passage leads to speculation that it may have been an extract from a much larger collection (did she really have so little to say?!), or maybe these sayings were specially chosen as they accord well with other sayings in Proverbs. What she did tell Lemuel was sensible and relevant enough to be recorded for others to learn from.

It seems that Lemuel was a very special son to her. Verse 2 indicates that he was in some way an answer to her prayers. Whether she had been unable to conceive for a long time, and that this was similar to Samuel being the answer to Hannah's prayer in 1 Samuel chapter 1, is not stated. What is clear from verse 2 is her passionate concern for the success of his reign. Her thrice repeated 'Listen!' shows an urgent desire to get his attention, as well as her anxiety that she will say the right thing to him. It also shows how much she cares for him. In fact, in the Hebrew text, the word she uses is not really 'Listen!' Rather this short word (*mah*) is an expression such as 'O', 'What' or 'How'. It is as though she is repeatedly calling out, 'O my son!' One full translation of this verse could be, 'What, my son, and what, the son of my womb, and what, son of my vows?' Essentially, she is crying out, perhaps mainly to herself, 'What shall I say to you, my son, now you are king; how shall I speak; what advice shall I give to you?'

The answer to this is found in verse 3 onwards, and consists of advice on what not to do! She realises the greatest threat to the stability of the throne does not come from ambitious internal rivals or external hostile nations, but from within the king himself, in particular the temptations to which he will be readily and regularly exposed.

Her plea to her son is not to spend his time or strength on wine and women (apparently songs are ok!). Extra wives and concubines had often brought trouble for kings in the past. As for wine and strong drink, it can give you a taste for more until eventually you start to crave it. Continual drinking can become a way of life for those at the top, but it brings two problems. It dulls the memory and clouds your judgement. This would harm a king's ability to govern fairly on behalf of all, particularly to uphold the rights of the oppressed and those unable to defend themselves, whether through ignorance or because they are too poor to hire someone to do this for them. Carrying out such responsibilities according to God's law is a test of kingship. A king who wastes his time and energy on women and wine may not be in a fit state or alert enough to perform these duties properly.

Perhaps verses 6-7 are meant to be taken cynically rather than seriously. Those who are poor and miserable can indulge in drink and drown their sorrows. It might even do them some good. It can't hurt them further; they are already at rock bottom. The king, on the other hand, the man at the top, has no such need and must not follow suit.

The second part of chapter 31, verses 10-31, contains what is known as an acrostic, an alphabetical poem where each verse begins with a successive letter of the Hebrew alphabet. The acrostic is quite common in the poetry books of the Hebrew Scriptures. For instance, there are nine examples of various kinds in the Psalms (Ps. 9, 10, 25, 34, 37, 111, 112, 119, 145). Some are quite straightforward in their form, others more complex. The book of Lamentations also relies heavily on this poetic form. Chapters 1, 2 and 4 are simple acrostics, whereas chapter 3 has a more complex triple form.

The Hebrew alphabet has 22 letters, so a simple acrostic will have 22 verses, as does our example in Proverbs 31:10-31. But the format can be developed and extended, as shown by some of the other examples mentioned above. However, even composing a simple acrostic takes a lot of thought and dedication to keep the progression going while making sense of what you are wanting to say.

Being an acrostic means this final part of Proverbs is quite different from everything that goes before, but overall it provides a fitting and satisfying conclusion to the whole book as it contains a practical illustration of the outworking of wisdom, and within a family context. Incidentally, the Septuagint version of the Old Testament separates the two portions of Proverbs 31, placing verses 1-9 after the end of chapter 24 and before the second collection of Solomon. It does, however, leave verses 10-31 to conclude the whole book, which also serves to indicate that this is a stand-alone anonymous poem rather than any possible continuation of the advice given to King Lemuel.

The subject of this poem is described at the beginning as 'A wife of noble character' (v10). Here is the complete wife, some might say the perfect wife, displaying as she does the full A to Z (or should we say Aleph to Tav?) of wisdom's virtues and rewards. Surely this must be Lady Wisdom herself (see chapter 9)? But not so. This is a real human being. She has a husband. Moreover, the phrase 'A wife of noble character' has occurred earlier in Proverbs, in 12:4, and was a real person there. So this is not a personification of wisdom, rather a human embodiment of what wisdom can be like in practice.

But she still seems too good to be true! Verse 10 warns us that she is difficult to find, perhaps even impossible. Clearly she is exceptionally gifted and privileged. She leaves nothing to chance. She has an amazing ability to organise everything. She has skill in many areas, including an acute business sense. Every minute of her time is given over to creating a household where nothing is second-rate. These are the disciplined qualities that make for stability and success in life. How she became so remarkable is not explained. We are to assume it must be because she has followed the path of wisdom all her life. That is the only way she could have become so successful. So this poem not only praises her but also extols the way of wisdom. It acts as a summary of the life of the wise in general, spurring us all on to gain wisdom in the way commended throughout the whole book.

From the poem itself we learn much about this splendid wife. She comes from a well-to-do family with servant girls (v15), but does not take advantage of this to live a life of leisure. She is industrious and works hard to provide for her family while still finding time to serve the poor and needy in the community (v20). She dresses well in fine linen and purple (v22) and makes warm clothes for her family. She is the wife of a city elder (v23), a prominent and well-respected citizen who makes important decisions on behalf of others. She has herself been well educated and is fully acquainted with wisdom (v26). In the final portion, verses 28-31, we see she is well thought of by her family and deserving of high praise. But it is verse 30 that is key to all this. What is the basis of her wisdom, hard work and noble character? As always in Proverbs, it is the fear of the Lord. And so as the book closes, we are reminded of how it opened, in 1:7. Here again is the theme which unifies the book despite the diversity within it.

Chapter Thirteen

Preaching from the Book of Proverbs

In this chapter we conclude our specific studies in the book of Proverbs by considering how this particular biblical book can, and should, be used in preaching, teaching and personal devotions.

It is fair to say that Proverbs is rarely taken as a preaching series. It is not impossible to do so, but as a book it does not easily lend itself to a chapter-by-chapter, verse-by-verse exposition. Perhaps a better way is to search out a selection of proverbs that could be brought into a different preaching series in order to illustrate the points being made there. If the main series is more doctrinal or theological in nature, then the occasional use of some proverbs could be beneficial in reinforcing the message in a practical way, or even in bringing some light relief, and a smile, to an otherwise more intense message.

While using the book of Proverbs in the pulpit is problematic and limited, it is ideal for group discussions or personal study. Here, in no particular order, are some thoughts on how to do this.

Overall, Proverbs should be read and discussed as part of the Word of God, not merely as the maxims and sayings of men and their wisdom. Passages about the nature and origin of wisdom, such as chapter 8, should be to the fore, as should those oft-repeated phrases about the fear of the Lord. It should also be remembered that Proverbs is part of the unfolding, progressive revelation of God, and that more wisdom was to come in the New Testament and from Christ himself. However, this does not mean we can dismiss these proverbs as irrelevant or outdated. In the past God spoke to his people in many and various ways (see Heb. 1:1), and this was one of them.

The book of Proverbs is a depository of treasure with all kinds of applications for daily life. We like this book as it is straightforward and accessible. However, it does need to be approached from the perspective of sharing in God's wisdom. These pieces of everyday advice, however down-to-earth, come from the mind of God.

The book of Proverbs also exercises a moral authority. It does this not by providing more laws and commands, but by reinforcing those already known. When reading a proverb it is always worth thinking whether it relates back to any particular law and how it might help illustrate its meaning. Proverbs also shows us that moral wisdom is often best passed on through persistent persuasion and personal example rather than by direct commands. Simple illustrations and humorous stories can often do the job just as well as strict laws. Perhaps there is something to learn from this when seeking to inform and influence others, especially our own children?

Proverbs is a unique book which makes a special contribution to the overall biblical story of man and God. It leaves the bigger messages about sin and salvation to others, focusing instead on how to live out our faith within God's kingdom and in this world. It is often quite earthy, rather than spiritual. Proverbs showed the Jewish people how to be faithful Jews when not engaged in specific religious activity, when not in the synagogue or the Temple. We should ask how these proverbs can help us be better Christians in our daily lives, when not in church meetings or fellowship groups. Proverbs act like mirrors. We should look for ourselves in each one. Here is a chance to be honest about ourselves. Does this mean me?

When reading through some proverbs, either individually or as a group, there are certain questions that can be asked of each proverb. Is there anything to avoid? Is there anything specifically to do? Is there anything God says he likes, or dislikes? What does it say about his nature or his will? Also, look for one thing that makes you laugh or smile, one thing that makes you think more deeply or even puzzles you. Above all, ask why this is 'wisdom'? Where actually is the wisdom in this proverb, and how does it manifest itself?

We may still wonder whether such a miscellany of short sayings is worth reading at all. But we read them all now so that they are in our minds for that one time when one proverb becomes relevant to our situation. This means not just glancing over them but spending time thinking them through so that they have sunk into our memory in readiness. Moreover, there is also a broader principle at work here, namely that we are being invited to join with the wise men of the past in developing our view of reality for today. Will we stand with the wise man or fall with the fool?

Chapter Fourteen

Job: An Introduction

In this general introduction to the book of Job we will discuss several preliminary questions before in later chapters we delve into some of the more challenging issues the book presents.

In the letter of James, the one book in the New Testament commonly regarded as a wisdom book, we read, 'You have heard of Job's perseverance' (Jas 5:11) and we certainly have. It's almost proverbial, though we usually tend to know it as the patience of Job. But hearing about his patience is one thing. Reading the whole book is another. And understanding its role within the wisdom literature of the Old Testament is yet another altogether.

There is a considerable contrast between Proverbs and Job. While Proverbs is appealing, Job is appalling, even horrific, especially at the start. Proverbs is often amusing, whereas Job, let's face it, can at times be boring. Proverbs is straightforward, containing mainly single sentences; Job is complex and often confusing with its many long dialogues and incessant debates. Here is chapter after chapter of seemingly endless verbiage. It's no surprise that people often give up on reading it all through or skim through certain parts of it.

In fact, Job is not read that often in Judaism either, certainly not publicly. This book is part of the Writings section of their scriptures, which means it belongs to the third category of the Tanak below the Torah and the Prophets. As such it does not feature in their regular synagogue readings. Nor is it read annually at the feasts, as are some of the other books in the Writings, though parts may be quoted at funerals and times of mourning. For instance, some Sephardic Jews hold public readings of Job on Tisha b'Av, the day of mourning over the destruction of both the first and second Temples.

We may also find ourselves wondering why Job is known as a wisdom book. How can this book teach us wisdom, especially if it differs so much from Proverbs? But in Job there is a facet of wisdom altogether different from that in Proverbs. These two books may seem at odds with each other, but we must remember that while Proverbs covers all of life, Job tackles just one question, albeit a big one: why do good people suffer? Job is therefore more philosophical in its approach and sceptical in its outlook. It is prepared to ask disturbing questions and push at the boundaries of traditional thinking. Hence it has a different role within the wisdom literature of the Old Testament to that of Proverbs, and at times will challenge the simple generalities and confident answers found in that book.

Wisdom on the whole tells us that life is moral, and that we will be happier and healthier if we follow its guidelines. But there will always be exceptions that need to be explored. Proverbs may occasionally add a cautionary word about the limits of wisdom and how much we can really understand of life, but in Job we are confronted with a torrent of demanding questions. Moreover, we must realise that calling Job a wisdom book doesn't mean that every statement in the book is wise, or even correct. Rather this is about wrestling with ideas and pursuing the search for wisdom in extreme circumstances. Job is a book which asks what wisdom is and where it can be found.

The book of Job has been called the most difficult book of the Bible. Certainly its message is not always easy to grasp. At times the text itself is difficult as it contains several words which occur nowhere else, thus making its meaning more obscure. But it is also a remarkable book and recognised as literature of a very high quality. Thomas Carlyle, a British essayist, historian and philosopher, thought there was nothing of equal literary merit inside or outside the Bible. He called it 'one of the grandest things ever written with the pen'. And the renowned Poet Laureate Alfred, Lord Tennyson famously referred to it as the greatest poem of ancient or modern times.

As for the structure of the book of Job, this is quite straightforward. In basic terms it has a prologue in prose (chapters 1-2) and an epilogue also in prose (42:7-17), between which comes a lengthy section of poetry (3:1–42:6). This prose-poetry-prose format is by no means unique to Job and has been found in other literature of the Ancient Near East, though not usually in such unbalanced proportions.

Further analysis is equally easy to discern. The central poetic section has its own clear structure. Job's lament in chapter 3 is followed by three rounds of speeches in chapters 4 to 27 and a wisdom poem in chapter 28. After this comes Job's final defence in chapters 29 to 31, a lengthy speech in chapters 32 to 37 by Elihu, a late newcomer on the scene, and finally a dramatic intervention by God in chapters 38 to 41, to which Job responds in chapter 42:1-6.

But if we dissect further the three rounds of speeches in chapters 4 to 27 we discover a strange feature. The first two cycles are consistent. In each case Eliphaz speaks first and Job replies, then Bildad delivers his speech to which Job responds, and finally Zophar speaks before Job replies to that. The third cycle begins in the same fashion but is truncated. Eliphaz starts off as usual, in chapter 22, and Job responds in chapters 23 to 24. But when Bildad begins his third speech he is cut short by Job after just six verses! And Zophar never gets a chance to complete the third cycle. His expected third speech is missing altogether.

Although we might be grateful to be spared yet more speeches of the same kind, this does create an interesting puzzle, which we will pick up later. Another poser is the mysterious late arrival of Elihu who says a lot but adds very little, before, at last, God breaks his silence in a magnificent climax. All these elements deserve further consideration later.

One obvious question for now is to ask who Job was. Was he a real historical person or a literary creation, invented for the purpose of this particular wisdom debate? There is another reference to Job in the Old Testament. In Ezekiel chapter 14 verses 14 and 20, he is linked with Noah and Daniel as one of three particularly righteous or faithful people. This may or may not be that helpful in deciding if Job actually existed. Nor are other Jewish writings that decisive either, despite much debate on the matter. The Talmud suggests the story of Job is just a parable, while later Jewish scholars insist that Job is not an imaginary person but a real human being, as were also his three friends. So overall, although a minority still regard Job as a fictional character, the main presumption nowadays is that he was an actual historical figure.

What about the setting for the book? Does this help us identify Job in any way? We are told in the opening verse that Job lived in the land of Uz, which is also mentioned in Jeremiah 25:20 and Lamentations 4:21. The actual location remains uncertain but there are some clues. It had to be reasonably accessible to the Sabean and Chaldean raiders in 1:15-17, and also for Job's friends to be able to visit him. Eliphaz came from Teman in northern Edom, and Bildad from Shuah, somewhere in Arabia. Given all this and that Lamentations 4:21 refers to 'Daughter Edom, you who live in the land of Uz', it seems the most likely region for Uz would be where Arabia bordered Edom or just inside Edom itself. From this we can conclude that Job was not an Israelite, which concurs with the fact that the text itself nowhere suggests that he was. In fact, it is likely he lived well before Israel became a nation.

Job seems to inhabit a very early period, that of the time of the patriarchs or even earlier. He resembles Abraham in how his wealth is measured. Also, like Abraham, he offers his own sacrifices (1:5), which means he existed before there was any official priesthood. Moreover, the book contains no reference to the covenants God made with Abraham or Moses, nor does it speak of the Exodus or the Law given at Sinai. These notable historical events are usually mentioned in later books, so their absence in Job is striking. One final point is that Job lived to a great age. At the end of the book we learn that he lived a further 140 years (42:16), giving him the kind of overall life-span more usual in the patriarchal period or just before.

So the historical setting of the book may be very early, but this does not necessarily mean the book itself is an early composition. The time when a story is actually written down may be much later than the time in which it is set. When it comes to dating the book of Job, scholars have produced a wide range of possibilities spreading across 2,000 years, from the pre-patriarchal time of the story itself to the first century BC. Mostly, though, the consensus has narrowed this down to sometime between the seventh and third centuries BC, the most common view being the sixth century BC. Various reasons support this. Literary affinities with the Psalms and Proverbs suggest Job must be later than the early monarchy (that is, the time of David and Solomon). Then there is the credible option that it was written during the exile as this was a time of great suffering for God's people.

However, trying to find a single date, or even a relatively narrow period of time, may not be the correct approach. It is more than likely that this work underwent transformation and development over time, rather than resulting from a single author at one particular moment in time. It is quite plausible that the original story of Job was known in traditional folk tale form from a very early stage. After all, the problem it discusses is one of the oldest in human history. One proposition is that this initial material may have provided the prose sections at the start and end of our book of Job. This could have been seen as a fitting framework into which a series of poetic episodes could be inserted to create a longer and more involved work. Certain features support this idea. For instance, experts report that the prose sections are in a more classical form of Hebrew which goes back to around the time of Abraham, while the poetic elements have characteristics which suggest they come from a later period.

Overall, the composition of the book and how it arrived in its final form can be left for scholars to debate. For us, it doesn't matter how it became the book we have in our Bibles today. The process may have involved some, even several, later poetic additions to an original prose story, but that doesn't affect its message to us now. As a person, Job is placed outside Israel, both geographically and chronologically, so the book transcends any historical origin or setting. Its purpose is timeless, its relevance is universal.

But we can still ask what kind of book we really have here? And does it depict events that actually happened? Is it fact, fiction, or a strange mixture called faction? It can certainly seem fictitious in places. At the start, four disasters come one after the other in rapid succession, while the ending has a 'happily ever after' feel to it. Above all, people don't usually sit around and speak in high quality poetry for hours on end while debating such traumatic issues. It all seems a bit artificial.

The solution to all this is to realise that what we have presented to us in the book of Job is more than just a debate, it is a drama. Behind this is a real person and real events. Something like this did happen in the past, but it has been dramatised in a particular way to bring out its full meaning and impact. Here is a story of old, not so much written down at the time, as written up later, long after the events it describes, and set in poetic form. We are familiar with such dramas. For instance we may enjoy a play like Shakespeare's Julius Caesar, without worrying about the fact that Caesar did not speak Shakespearian English. We allow for poetic licence!

Job may not be the sort of theatrical experience we would choose to go to today, but it fits what we read in the book. Experts in these matters say the book has an underlying plot whose development gives coherence to the book as a whole. The cycles and sections are skilfully assembled to work together in a series of tempo changes and dramatic tensions, leading from climax to climax until the final resolution bursts upon us. Admittedly, this may not be apparent to most of us and reading it can remain a real test of our own patience and perseverance.

However, if it is correct to consider the book of Job as a drama, then firstly we ought to meet the full cast of characters and see what happens when the curtain rises. This we will do in our next chapter.

Chapter Fifteen

Job: Meet the Cast

In the last chapter we began to examine the book of Job, concluding that what is presented to us here is a drama. So let's meet the cast in order of appearance.

We start with the title character, Job himself. We mentioned some details about him in our last chapter, that he was a non-Israelite living in the land of Uz around the time of the patriarchs or earlier. Now, as the book opens, we find a character reference. We notice he feared God, a key requirement of biblical wisdom, which also explains why he shunned evil. He is described as blameless and upright, indicating his integrity and that he fulfilled God's requirements in caring for the poor and needy, and that he was fair in his dealings with his servants.

This is an impressive tribute but does not mean he was without sin at all. Indeed he does not claim to be sinless (7:21, 13:26, 14:16-17) but he does profess his innocence (9:15, 20, 10:15), meaning that within what was understood about rewards and punishment at the time, he didn't deserve suffering on this scale. What is also being established here at the outset is that if Job is faced with senseless suffering that he cannot understand, then we should not expect an easy answer either. There will be nothing trivial in what we are about to read.

Job is extremely wealthy, the greatest of all in that region (1:3). He is a landowner and farmer (1:14, 31:38-40), as well as being a city elder (29:7), making him a semi-nomadic chieftain. This is not an unusual combination as leaders of a tribe often adopted a more settled lifestyle while the rest of their people remained pastoral nomads.

Our second main character is God himself who, although he does not feature throughout the whole book, has a key role in the opening scene and again later towards the end. This is clearly Yahweh but as this personal name was not revealed until the time of Moses, the terms used in Job are Eloah (El, Elohim) and Shaddai. The former is usually translated 'God', the latter as 'Almighty', a title that occurs some thirty times in Job but not often elsewhere. He is depicted as a great king within a heavenly court, surrounded by angelic courtiers, more properly described as 'sons of Elohim'. They are mentioned again later in Job as having rejoiced at the time of creation (38:7). The theology of angelic beings was rather patchy at that time, becoming more developed in the period between the Old and New Testaments, but here they are presented as being his messengers and servants, and among them is our next character, the satan.

We refer to him as 'the satan' as this is how he is described in the Hebrew text, with the definite article attached, and how we should understand him in this passage. In Hebrew, 'satan' is a word which means 'accuser' or 'adversary' or 'prosecutor'. The word occurs a few times in the Old Testament (see Zech. 3:1-2, Ps. 109:6, 1 Chr. 21:1). In each case it is a title not a proper name. At this point in biblical revelation it designated a function or role rather than a particular person, so we should not assume that 'the satan' in Job is the same creature known as the devil or Satan in the New Testament. Here in Job, he simply appears alongside the other 'sons of God', one of many beings under God's authority within the angelic court. This creature is not an equal with God. He is part of God's creation, as are all supernatural beings.

However, he does seem to have a specific task, roaming the earth as a sort of investigator or special reporter. But what is revealed about him is hardly in keeping with what we would expect of a true servant of God. He displays malevolence against Job and wants to prove him to be a hypocrite. He can't believe someone would love God for his own sake, or serve him without reward and blessings in return. He argues with God, challenges him and casts doubt on his judgement. Overall, the picture we have of this satan is complex and rather ambivalent but it is fair to say that, at the very least, he seems to pre-figure the Satan we meet in the gospels, and that it was inevitable the devil should be given that title par excellence. If this is a little off-putting, we should remember that the Hebrew word for 'messiah' (*mashiach*), meaning 'anointed one', also went through the same process. It described others who served God's purposes before it became part of how we think of Jesus as Messiah or the Christ.

A vital point about this 'satan' figure in Job is that after the first two chapters he disappears entirely from the book. He is irrelevant to all subsequent discussions. No one mentions him at all, not even God at the end. He does not reappear as we might expect in the epilogue. So we cannot conclude the main point of the book is to solve the problem of suffering with 'satan' in mind. We cannot conclude that it was all his doing. The book of Job does not allow us to attribute all suffering to the work of this 'satan' or any other.

The next character on our list is Job's wife, who makes a cameo appearance. She is not named in the text, though one Jewish tradition says she is Dinah, Jacob's only daughter, but this is difficult to sustain. Despite having only a single line in the story, in 2:9, she is quite unforgettable. She seems to be asking her husband whether he is intending to cling on to his claim of innocence. Do you still think this way? You must have done something wrong! As such, she pre-figures the speeches of those who will appear on stage soon.

The rest of her statement is usually translated, 'Curse God and die!' This is a correct translation even though the Hebrew word is actually *barech*, which means bless. However, this word can be used ironically or euphemistically to mean the very opposite, especially when referring to God. Rather than curse God directly, you would say 'bless' even if that is not your intention. The actual Hebrew word for curse is first used in Job in 3:1 when he curses the day of his birth. It may be unsettling to think of Job's wife pressing him to curse God for his predicament, but equally disturbing is her wish for him to commit suicide and end it all, as though he has nothing good left to live for at all, including herself. Does this reflect her own sense of self-worth?

Job's response is to call her foolish which, as we have seen before, does not mean stupid but morally deficient. She lacks wisdom and her statements reflect this. But before we judge her too harshly let us remember she is also suffering in all this, especially over the loss of her own children. After this brief appearance in the prologue, she leaves the stage and plays no further part in the drama that unfolds.

We turn now to Job's three friends, who each make a long journey from their own homes. It seems they first meet up together and agree to visit Job to 'sympathise with him and comfort him' (2:11).

Eliphaz is the oldest of the three friends and the gentlest in his approach to Job. He piously holds on to the orthodox position of rewards and punishment. The accumulated wisdom of the ages is that suffering is due to sin and so must be true in Job's case. He urges Job to accept this in humility. Repent and all will be OK. When Job doesn't admit to this, Eliphaz accuses him of being obstinate, and starts to use sarcasm and scorn. During his first speech he relates a strange spiritual experience he once had, which he uses to confirm his view (4:12-21). He also applies logic in his arguments. Either Job is unrighteous and deserves to suffer or God is unrighteous in making Job suffer. The latter is unthinkable so the former must be true.

Bildad is another traditionalist, full of jargon and clichés, but less sensitive and compassionate than Eliphaz. He gets angry and soon runs out of patience, becoming exasperated with Job. He tells him to stop arguing with

God who must be right. Bildad appeals to tradition (8:8-10), but his approach is flawed in that the truths he draws from the past do not fit this particular case. In the end he has no better advice for Job than does Eliphaz.

Zophar is the youngest but is also rigid in his views and blunt in how he expresses them. He accuses Job of avoiding the issue. He should stop talking and start confessing. If he hasn't sinned consciously then he must have sinned unconsciously. God knows everything and has already been lenient in overlooking some of Job's sins (11:6). Despite all this, Zophar, to his credit, is wise enough to pose the questions that matter most in this particular discussion. 'Can you fathom the mysteries of God? Can you probe the limits of the Almighty?' (11:7). Zophar seems to be ahead of the others in this respect.

Our final character doesn't come onto the scene until well into the second half of the drama. Elihu is the youngest of them all. He has waited his turn, respecting his elders and politely listening to those who should be wiser than him. But all the time he has been growing impatient with their arguments and when he does speak it is out of anger (32:2-5). He rebukes them all, including Job, arrogantly telling him to be quiet and pay attention to him. 'Be silent, and I will teach you wisdom' (33:33). With the confidence of youth, he reckons he has all the answers. He knows God's mind better than the others and can speak with insight and wisdom derived from the spirit within him (32:8, 18, 33:4). Some commentators see a hidden meaning in 32:18. The word 'spirit' can also mean 'wind', so is this verse implying he is just a windbag?! Certainly, for all his many words, he adds very little to the debate. He accuses Job of sin and says he must be guilty in some way, but this merely echoes what others have repeatedly said.

Elihu is a puzzling character. He has a Hebrew name which means 'He is my God', and his four speeches are joined together without any response between (chapters 32–33, 34, 35, 36–37). Job certainly never bothers to answer him. After he has spoken, Elihu disappears from the scene as quickly as he came. He is not even mentioned in the epilogue when God rebukes Job's friends. Some commentators think Elihu is sent by God to supply the trial Job demands but which God himself cannot be expected to provide. Others suggest the portrayal of Elihu is a satirical caricature of a brash, opinionated young man, bringing light relief before the dramatic climax. Others take a more sympathetic attitude. He tries hard but with limited success. We will discuss further his literary role within the whole drama later.

Meanwhile, we will examine how the drama begins. At the start two plots are interwoven. The prologue alternates between earth and heaven but always keeping them separate. The heavenly storyline is known only to us, the readers (or audience), not to any of the characters involved in the earthly part of the story. This creates a dramatic tension by letting us into knowledge that others will never know. Nor indeed do they ever find out, not even towards the end when God speaks, nor in the epilogue when final resolution occurs.

Although it is tempting to draw theological theories from the first two chapters, we should realise they are primarily a literary device designed to create a scenario for what is to follow. We are not being shown a typical day in heaven.

Rather, we learn that God approves of Job and is confident in his faith and that he will be able to stand such testing. But Job does not know this, which is crucial to the whole story. The really big question is found in 1:9, 'Does Job fear God for nothing?' In other words, can humans have a disinterested faith in God, one without reference to any rewards and punishments? Here is a challenge for all of us to debate. Also within these opening chapters we learn that innocent suffering can exist, including extreme suffering which is truly undeserved. So when later Job insists his suffering is not due to any sin on his part, we know this is true. Thus informed we can move on into the rest of the drama.

At this point, three of Job's friends appear. They had heard of his traumatic experiences, but when they see him they are shocked and deeply saddened. Together they sit in silence for seven days. This is thought to be the origin of the Jewish cultural practice of sitting *shiva*. When a person is in a period of grieving, friends come to sit with them, but out of consideration for their loss do not engage in conversation until spoken to. Here in Job, the friends wait for him to speak first, which will then allow them to express their views. When Job does eventually break the silence, he starts by cursing the day of his birth, wishing he had never been born. Thus begins a lengthy and at times heated debate, which we pick up in our next chapter.

Chapter Sixteen

Job:
Going Round in Cycles

So far, we have said that one way of studying the book of Job is as a drama being played out, and in the last chapter we met the cast. Now it is time to let the drama unfold.

After sitting in absolute silence for seven days with his three friends, Job at last breaks that silence with an outpouring of anguished statements and questions as he tries to make sense of what has happened to him (chapter 3). He is not directly addressing the others at this point but his words open up the situation for them to respond and give them permission to make their own contributions to the debate. After which, nothing holds them back!

It is quite likely they had been Job's friends for some time and were well known to each other. Maybe they were all wealthy rulers with shared backgrounds and lifestyles. It is possible they had met many times before and often talked about life's difficulties, but now there was an urgency to their discussion provided by a real-life context.

We won't be commenting on all that they said or undertake a speech-by-speech analysis. Commentaries can provide that. Rather we will try to understand what is happening in general.

One by one, the three friends, each in his own way, rebuke Job for his supposed sin and urge him to repent in order to be restored. Even if Job doesn't know what he's done wrong he might as well repent. We are all sinners anyway so it won't hurt to confess something! But Job will not accept easy answers to his situation. Boldly he speaks his mind, constantly declaring he is innocent. All this has set up a tense, if somewhat prolonged, drama. How will this quarrel eventually end?

Eliphaz, Bildad and Zophar, in one way or another, all adhere to the traditional wisdom of the time, one which upheld an idealised world of prosperous saints and destitute sinners, without exceptions. They assume suffering implies guilt of some kind and employ a pattern of reasoning often used in Proverbs. Eliphaz in particular seems capable of speaking in such terms: 'Blessed is the man whom God corrects; so do not despise the discipline of the Almighty' (5:17; also v18-26). He ends his first speech by declaring: 'We have examined this, and it is true. So hear it and apply it to yourself' (5:27). In short, they all agree on their advice to Job – confess and be blessed!

The slight variations in their individual arguments perhaps reflect different strands or schools of this traditional wisdom, but essentially there is nothing new in what they say. Their views are those that could have been heard elsewhere. They are simply echoing the beliefs of those who at that time were deemed to be 'wise'. The cycles of speeches are repetitious because the friends are stuck in their views. So when their initial admonitions don't work, the three antagonists can't change tack. They simply go from gentle probing for hidden sin to stern rebukes regarding the same.

The end result is that these repeated cycles create plenty of heat but no real light. Job keeps fighting back but no-one comes out a winner. It all remains in unresolved tension, which makes for good drama.

It should be recognised that the three friends are not hypocrites or heretics. They are firm believers in a God who is all powerful and all just. They may represent 'old school' wisdom, and be somewhat arrogant in their pontification, nevertheless the truth they espouse is correct. But it is only partial truth. Their knowledge is incomplete. If they (and indeed the book of Proverbs) provided a full understanding of all reality then innocent suffering would be incomprehensible. The point behind these speeches is that, because they don't yet know enough, their application to Job's situation is faulty.

The central theme of the book of Job is the suffering of a righteous man, but this does not mean its main purpose is to give us an answer to the problem. Its length and form seem to increase the tension of the problem not resolve it. In fact, from our point of view, as readers, the prologue already gives us some of the answer, or at least enough for the purposes of the drama. The dialogue which follows relies upon us knowing why Job suffers while realising that he has no such knowledge. We should also appreciate that Job's real suffering is not just in his losses and illness but that these experiences do not conform to his own ideas, those he has been brought up to believe in. Suddenly he is cast adrift, rudderless in an uncharted sea, his former beliefs no longer any use. He understands very well this wisdom that his friends are repeating to him, but he also now knows that it no longer seems to work. That can only add to his anguish.

One issue with the speeches we mentioned earlier is that the third cycle is incomplete. Bildad says very little and Zophar has no third speech at all. The pattern has broken down. Scholars have suggested several reasons for this. One is that this was what the author intended and that there are good dramatic reasons behind his shortening of the third cycle. Another is that the original text was once complete but some portions became lost or even rearranged, so that the rest of what was spoken by Bildad plus Zophar's missing speech is now to be found in Job's comments in chapters 26 and 27.

Underpinning this latter view is that much of what Job says in these chapters runs counter to his previous comments. We would expect consistency of thought from all the debaters and during this cycle Job appears to contradict his earlier statements and begin to argue like his friends, only to defiantly reject them again later. So some scholars propose assigning 26:5-14 to Bildad, and 27:13-23 to Zophar, though some allocate these verses also to Bildad with Zophar remaining speechless. Several more rearrangements have been attempted in an effort to recover a better order and rebalance the cycles, but overall none are satisfying and such reconstruction could involve a more drastic rearrangement of the text than it can realistically sustain.

Nevertheless, many maintain that the text has suffered disruption and dislocation in some way, though we may challenge this by asking why the last cycle should be like the other two at all. It is perfectly natural for the third cycle to break down at this point. The debate has become increasingly frustrating and meaningless. It has started to collapse under the weight of excessive repetition, so it is pointless to continue any longer. Bildad simply dries up while Zophar shrugs his shoulders and gives up in exasperation. Why go on?

This is a plausible scenario within the whole dramatic presentation, but it still leaves the issue of the inconsistency of Job's arguments found within chapters 26 and 27, which many scholars say remains unacceptable. So there is a further refinement to the view that the text we have today is indeed the original one. Job now finds Bildad extremely tiresome and so he impatiently and sarcastically cuts him short (26:2-4). He then mimics Bildad, completing his argument for him in the rest of chapter 26. He then does the same thing in chapter 27 regarding what Zophar might be about to say. They have repeated themselves so much that Job has their arguments off by heart and can reproduce them himself. If this is what is happening, then these are not Job's own views and hence he is not being inconsistent with what he said before. Moreover, this tactic silences them forever. When Job can say their pieces for them, they all know the debate is over. Thankfully, there cannot be a fourth cycle!

Throughout the cycles of speeches Job has become increasingly irritated and indignant. His protests have grown in intensity, though he never reacted as the 'satan' had hoped for. In chapters 29 to 31 he continues to lament over his current misery and longs nostalgically for his previous happiness. He also makes his final defence of innocence. He has examined himself thoroughly and his conscience is clear. He has no reason to think he has done wrong, so in 31:35 he declares that he is ready to be judged, and calls for the trial to begin, certain that he will be acquitted. He signs off his defence and rests his case, and so in 31:40 we read, 'The words of Job are ended.'

Having reached a climax at 31:35 with Job challenging the Almighty to answer him, what happens next is very strange. Instead of the Almighty we get Elihu, a totally new player in our drama. We have already met Elihu as part of the cast. We said then he was a puzzling character. We will now discuss his role within the book of Job.

In effect we have one long speech by Elihu lasting six chapters, but it is also four separate speeches joined together with no response between (chapters 32–33, 34, 35, 36–37). Here again is another challenge for scholars. Many speculate whether this was a later interpolation rather than part of the original text. It is in a slightly different style from the rest of the book and its literary quality is inferior. Moreover, Elihu appears on the scene out of nowhere, only to disappear again just as rapidly. He is not even mentioned in the epilogue when God rebukes the other three for their words. Perhaps he is to be ignored as irrelevant, not worth further comment?

Others argue that even if this section was a later addition, the differences in style are not enough to prove someone else was responsible for writing his part. In addition, Elihu often alludes to the debate already made, so if this is not the same author at work, it must be someone with a detailed understanding of the whole book and with sufficient skill to make Elihu appear integral to the text.

But the main issue with Elihu's speeches is that Job's final words (31:35ff) have set up an expectation that we will hear next from the Almighty himself. It all seems a bit of an anti-climax. And then when God does eventually speak (38:1ff), it is as if nothing has happened in between. The response of the Almighty has been delayed by yet another lengthy discourse that adds little, if anything, to the debate. So is it possible to find a positive role for Elihu within the drama?

Is he another protagonist, like the others? Or is he some kind of adjudicator, summing up and evaluating what has been said so far? If Elihu is attempting to be the arbiter Job has demanded, then he fails miserably. This would only serve to reiterate the point that no human can provide a satisfactory resolution to the debate, and would again prepare us for the Almighty to make his contribution.

One feature of Elihu's speeches is that as they progress they lay less stress on Job's suffering and more on God's majesty. Perhaps this is to prepare us for God's entrance into the drama. Indeed Elihu's final words (37:14ff) can be seen as pre-echoing God himself. Moreover, as Elihu comes towards the end of his discourse, a storm gathers (36:27–37:13). Whether literally or poetically, it prefigures the storm out of which God makes his appearance and his judgement. Overall, Elihu may add little to the debate but much to the drama. His appearance does not weaken the dramatic sequence by interrupting it. Rather by keeping apart Job's challenge and God's response, it generates a new tension. As an interlude, it creates suspense, after which the word of the Lord is all the more majestic.

However, it could still be argued that Elihu's speeches form the least needed section of the book, one that most would willingly cut from an already over-extended drama. Elihu may be a transitional figure fulfilling a key dramatic role, but it is fair to say that, after the great torrent of talk already endured, more human opinions are neither required nor desired at this point. Being kept waiting even longer for divine enlightenment might be seen as a delay too far.

At the risk of causing further delay ourselves, we will also postpone our consideration of God's intervention a little longer, as there is an important chapter we have omitted so far. Chapter 28 contains a magnificent poem on wisdom, and we will focus on this next.

Chapter Seventeen

Job: Chapter 28, A Wisdom Poem

Chapter 28 of the book of Job contains a magnificent poem on wisdom itself. It can be argued that this poem alone justifies placing the book of Job within the category of wisdom literature.

There are two aspects of this poem which are undisputed. One is that it is a masterpiece, a remarkable poetic exposition on the nature of wisdom and its inaccessibility to mere mortals via human effort. The other area of general agreement is that it stands back from the immediate debate and the arguments that have been raging. As such, it offers some respite from the strife, a chance to catch our breath before Job takes up the discourse again in chapters 29 to 31.

But there the scholarly consensus ends and the usual questions and disputes begin. For a start, should we really regard it as the central part of Job's lengthy discourse which runs from chapter 26 through to chapter 31? Or is it better to think of it as an independent poem added into the book at this point by whoever was compiling the final version? And if so, then why?

It is quite correct to comment, as many have done, that the poem seems rather out of place coming from the mouth of Job. The sudden change of tone and style is quite a surprise. It has a less combatant and more reflective mood which makes it noticeably different from the passionate outpourings of Job's previous speeches. It is calm and detached, out of keeping with the way Job is feeling at this point.

As an abstract contemplation on the theme of wisdom it is unrelated to what has gone before. It interrupts the flow created by the previous speeches and so is usually designated as an interlude between the main series of dialogues and Job's final word. It is therefore often considered to be an addition by the author himself, his own personal pronouncement rather than part of Job's speech.

To back this up, some point to 29:1, which says, 'Job continued his discourse', claiming this as evidence that he is picking up again from the end of chapter 27 after 'giving way' to the poetic interlude. However, this is inconclusive as the same phrase occurs at 27:1, which definitely follows straight on from Job's reply in chapter 26. Moreover, Elihu's long speech in chapters 32 to 37 is often punctuated with 'Then Elihu said' (34:1, 35:1) or 'Elihu continued' (36:1) without any suggestion there has been anything else added between. So on that basis, it remains possible to consider chapters 26 to 31 as one long speech by Job, though perhaps in three parts with chapter 28 offering something of a contrast to break up what might otherwise be considered rather monotonous.

Nevertheless, the issues of style and tone mentioned above remain strong and sufficiently valid to make it unlikely that this is part of Job's discourse. Overall, chapter 28 is best regarded as an intrusion, albeit a pleasant and worthwhile one. In which case, several more questions arise. Is it a later addition by another author? Or was it always part of the book with the original author adding something different at this point, perhaps to prepare for what he knows is coming in the rest of the drama?

The consequences of these two alternatives are quite significant. If it is a later addition then we can question whether it has been placed in the right setting in the book. If it is from the original author, then we are more likely to accept its current position. What can we say about these options?

There is no doubt that whatever its origin the poem can be treated as a freestanding piece and be studied separately without knowing anything about the rest of the book of Job. Detaching it from the book and contemplating its message in isolation can prove to be very fruitful and beneficial. However, discarding it completely, as some suggest, leaves the book much poorer.

The case for removing it entirely rests upon the view that it anticipates the divine speeches too soon, and so destroys the impact to come of God's intervention. Others counter this by saying that the opposite is true. It cleverly foreshadows his speeches, acting as a sort of pre-echo which enhances the effect of what God will say later. Indeed, it is argued, it shows the absolute need for the coming divine intervention by insisting on the limitations of human attempts to find wisdom for themselves. It seems you can make your own mind up on this matter! Perhaps the decisive point in all this should be the effect its inclusion or exclusion makes upon the drama as a whole. Cutting scenes from a play always needs careful thought.

But if it is to stay as part of the book, and assuming that it is a later addition by a different author, we can still ask if it can be placed elsewhere to better effect. Various options have emerged, some of which are familiar from similar discussions we have come across before. For instance, does it belong to Bildad's third speech, which is very short, or could it be Zophar's missing third speech? Others have suggested it should come after chapter 37, crowning what Elihu has brought to the debate; others still that it should somehow be included as part of God's speeches, perhaps because it seems more divinely inspired than anything the humans have come up with.

As none of these relocations seem to provide anything better overall, most scholars find no real objection to the poem's present setting. It serves its purpose well where it is by providing a much-appreciated respite from the long uninterrupted flow of arguments that started back in chapter 4. Some have compared its role to that of the chorus in Greek tragedy by which the author interjects his own comments upon the drama so far, though it should be remembered that such a literary device didn't appear until the fifth century BC. Perhaps it is best to see it as the curtain descending for a brief interval halfway through the drama, providing a formal closure to the preceding dialogues and a bridge to that still to come. Support for this comes from the reference to the fear of the Lord in its final verse (28:28), echoing, perhaps deliberately, the opening verse (1:1), thus forming a framework known as an *inclusio*. In literature, this involves starting and ending a section with the same word or phrase in order to create a sense of completeness or closure. In our case it serves to divide the book into two halves. Whether we regard chapter 28 as closing Act 1 (curtain down) or opening Act 2 (curtain up), it works either way.

After all this deliberation and speculation, it is time to investigate the content of chapter 28. Regardless of how this marvellous poem found its way into the drama or ended up in its present location, what is really important is its message. So what does it tell us?

The poem divides into three stanzas. The first of these, verses 1-11, relates how humans have successfully explored the depths of the earth in their search for precious metals and rare gems. When it comes to mining for gold, silver and other minerals, man has demonstrated great ingenuity and overcome many dangers, far more than encountered in harvesting the fields above ground. Also through his exploitation of the innermost recesses of the earth, man has shown himself to be far superior to the animals. However, the resource that man needs most of all is wisdom. It is worth far more than gold and precious jewels. But despite all of our considerable achievements, we remain unable to locate and obtain wisdom for ourselves. So in verse 12 comes the key question of the chapter: 'But where can wisdom be found? Where does understanding dwell?'

The second stanza, in verses 13-20, continues to extol the value of wisdom as being far greater than anything else we can find or own. But we are warned that it cannot be purchased with any of the treasures we already have, nor can it be obtained through great feats of human daring or imagination, or, we might add today, even via our modern marvels of technology. Nowadays, a list of man's greatest feats would include our exploration of space and the ocean depths, and our ability to probe the inner world of the atom. But how wise has all this made us? Have we found wisdom through these means?

So in verse 20 the same question is asked once more: 'Where then does wisdom come from? Where does understanding dwell?' This time there is an answer, in the third stanza (v21-28). Only God knows what true wisdom is and where it can be found. 'God understands the way to it and he alone knows where it dwells' (v23). This is because wisdom is the principle by which God gave order to the entire cosmos. In verse 27 we read that God 'looked at wisdom and appraised it; he confirmed it and tested it'. Then he revealed to the human race the answer to the twice-repeated question. 'The fear of the Lord – that is wisdom, and to shun evil is understanding' (v28).

It is no surprise to find here the customary theme of all wisdom literature, namely, the fear of the Lord. The point of Job chapter 28 is that God is the only source of the wisdom we seek. Only he can unlock that treasury, so we must ask him and this requires the right attitude towards him. In this sense, Job chapter 28 is already pointing ahead to what the New Testament will say about wisdom. It also has affinities with another wisdom poem, one we have already looked at in Proverbs chapter 8, but the difference is that whereas in Proverbs wisdom takes on the role of a personified figure, here in Job we have a testimony to God himself.

Whether or not Job chapter 28 is a separate poem inserted by an unknown hand, it takes us to the heart of the issue.

Will we accept wisdom from Almighty God or continue to strive for it by our own efforts and still not find it? Overall, the poem makes a strong comment on the debate so far and upon those involved in it, hinting at God's assessment of the three friends to come in 42:7-9. It also points ahead to the need for God to intervene in the debate. As we said earlier, it partly anticipates what God will say in the speeches of chapters 38 to 41, which we will turn to next.

Chapter Eighteen

Job: Chapters 38 to 42, And God Said . . .

We are currently working our way through the book of Job and have now reached the dramatic entry of the Almighty himself. We have waited a long time for this, as had Job. He had repeatedly asked God to speak to him (some say up to thirty-six times) and eventually God did, but perhaps not in the way Job expected.

God appears in a tempest or whirlwind not, as Job wished, in the calm of a courtroom. He speaks to Job 'out of the storm' (38:1), presumably the same storm that had been gathering during Elihu's speeches (36:27–37:13). Unless, that is, this is not a physical storm at all but refers instead to Job's internal tempest, the whirlwind of his thoughts, feelings and emotions which have dominated his state of mind throughout the drama. Perhaps God chose to speak to Job within his innermost being rather than via an external voice that was audible to the others. This was too personal for them to hear.

This is the only book in the biblical wisdom literature in which God does speak, and as usual scholars debate several unusual features about the speeches and come up with many views on these matters. For a start, there are two distinct speeches from the Lord (38:1–40:2, 40:6–41:34) with a short response from Job in between (40:3-5). But why is there a second speech at all? Didn't the first speech do enough to convince Job? What does the second speech add?

Scholars also find certain differences between these speeches which are puzzling. The first consists of several rapid sketches and is well written and constructed. The second is more ponderous and poetically inferior, with several strange elements such as the seemingly irrelevant extended examples of Behemoth and Leviathan. What are these creatures, and why does Job need to hear so much about them?

Equally baffling is that when God starts speaking he doesn't seem to answer Job's problems directly or even at all. He disregards Job's plight, ignores his claims of innocence and says nothing about why he has suffered so much. Nor does he address the wider question of why the innocent suffer, which we have been waiting for. It seems the answer is there is no answer.

We, as readers, still have the prologue to guide our thinking, but for Job and the other participants, that remains hidden. God brushes aside the debate completely, including the latest speeches of Elihu, and thunders in with a stream of rhetorical questions which must have sent Job's head spinning. Perhaps we are meant to conclude that the fact that God condescends to speak at all is a sufficient answer for Job. But the whole of the first speech comes across as a relentless grilling, a merciless pounding of someone already down. Is it God's intention to grind Job into the dust? We have called this chapter 'And God said . . .' Perhaps it should be entitled 'And God said *what*?'

While the style of the first speech may be intimidating and insistent, the content is engrossing and awe-inspiring. We, together with Job, are taken on a tour of creation from the farthest reaches of space, through the mighty seas and mountains, to the beasts and the birds, ending with the horse and the eagle. We are left in no doubt as to the power and majesty of the one who until now has remained silent and separate from the drama. Then, as a culmination of all this, Job is challenged to respond: 'Will the one who contends with the Almighty correct him? Let him who accuses God answer him!' (40:2).

Job's answer seems to be a humble capitulation (40:4-5). Battered into submission by the barrage of questions, he totally surrenders. Or at least that is the common view. Job has spoken out of turn. His speeches have been abrasive and arrogant. He has repeatedly accused God of doing him wrong (see especially chapters 19 and 27), so God has replied with a stinging rebuke. Who do you think you are to talk to me like that? I am the Almighty creator. You are a mere creature. All of God's questions have served to remind Job which one of them is God. At the same time he has been enlarging Job's thinking, highlighting not only the majesty of creation but also the mysteries it contains. Overall God may not be directly answering Job's questions, but by emphasising certain truths he is pointing him, and us, towards a new path of wisdom.

However, there might be more to Job's response in 40:4-5 than a complete surrender. It is possible, even likely, that he simply means he has nothing more to say, no further accusations to make, and so he is inviting God to continue. He will listen rather than continue to speak his mind. This resolves the issue of why there is a second speech at all and also helps explain the ultimate purpose of it. The second speech is only superfluous if Job's first response is a complete capitulation and that this was God's aim all along. But was it really God's intention to devastate Job in this way, or did he have a larger purpose in mind? If so, we are only halfway through.

To understand this better, notice that God starts in the same way in 40:7 as he did earlier in 38:3. Once more Job is told to 'gird up his loins' or 'brace himself' like a man. The Hebrew word for 'man' is *geber*, which can just mean a man generally but can also have vigorous connotations, referring to a valiant man or warrior. God wants Job to stand up and face his creator, not grovel on the ground. If God has overpowered Job, it is only temporary, and so that he can raise him up again even stronger. On this basis it becomes clear why God has to speak a second time. Job's response to the first speech, 'I will say no more' (40:5), is inadequate. God doesn't want Job to be silent. He wants to engage with Job in dialogue. 'You shall answer me' (40:7).

It can still be argued that Job had to submit fully and experience self-humbling before he could gain a deeper wisdom and reconnect with God again, but this second speech can also make God seem cruel by pursuing Job further than is called for. So how Job responds to this second speech will be important and we will study this in due course. But first we have to gird up our own loins and brace ourselves to meet two mighty monsters.

The second speech of God is nearly all about two strange creatures called Behemoth (40:15-24) and Leviathan (41:1-34). Who or what are they, and why are they important to what God is saying?

Some commentators look for these creatures within the existing animal kingdom. Behemoth is often equated to a hippopotamus and Leviathan to a crocodile, but generally this assumption doesn't work. There may be some physical similarities; for instance, Leviathan's teeth and solid scaly back (41:14-17) do suggest a crocodile, but it also has fire-breathing abilities (41:19-21), more like a dragon. Even if extravagant poetic language is being used then these beasts still seem to transcend ordinary terrestrial creatures.

What about the Hebrew words themselves? Do they give any clues? The word *leviathan* is from a root meaning to twist or coil, and so came to refer generally to a large sea monster, like a giant sea snake. The Hebrew *behemoth* is interesting in that it is a plural word. The singular, *behemah*, refers typically to a large, usually domesticated, land animal but tends to be used as a collective noun, for instance, cattle. So pluralising the word is unusual and may express something more extreme, a kind of mega monster, rather than offer a physical description of any known member of the animal kingdom.

From this we can see why many scholars believe these creatures are not so much zoological as mythological. In particular, they find similarities with several ancient creation myths, such as those of Mesopotamia and Babylon, which speak of chaos monsters that had to be subdued when their particular god created the world. This combat myth of creation was popular in the ancient world and, although very different from the account in Genesis, would be known to the Hebrew people at the time of Job. One example is in the Ugaritic Baal cycle, where a seven-headed dragon or serpent, known as Lotan or Litan, is defeated by the storm god Hadad-Ba'al. The verbal similarity between Lotan or Litan and Leviathan may suggest a link, as might its description as a serpent or dragon.

But caution is needed over making connections between these mythical creatures and those mentioned in scripture. For a start, neither Behemoth nor Leviathan are described in the Bible as being in conflict *with* God over creating the world. Rather, they were created *by* God. God says to Job, 'Look at Behemoth, which I made along with you' (Job 40:15). And Psalm 104:26 refers to Leviathan as one of the many sea creatures which God formed to frolic there.

Behemoth and Leviathan may seem fierce and potentially dangerous but there is no evidence they are aggressive or violent towards God. He did not have to subdue them. In fact, in these chapters in Job, God seems rather pleased with them as part of his creation and thinks positively of them. For instance, he praises the Leviathan as being without equal, as though he has royal status (41:33-34).

There is, however, one text in which the Leviathan is seen as God's enemy. In Isaiah 27:1, God will slay Leviathan, the gliding serpent, the coiling serpent, the monster of the sea. The context of 'In that day' suggests this is part of God's end-time victory over evil, so the conflict imagery is appropriate here. But in Job this is more complex.

Interpretations of the second speech usually reflect pre-determined ideas of how God is dealing with Job at this point. The standard view is that Job needed further telling off and humbling, so God calls on these fierce creatures to show his power. I have conquered and subdued them. You can't do this, Job, so how dare you question me? But, as we have seen, the idea of conflict between God and these monsters is not evident here, and wrong conclusions about this leads to incorrect theories on God's treatment of Job. So is there a better way of reading these chapters?

The point of this speech is not that God can subdue these creatures and Job can't, so he must capitulate in total surrender to God. Nor did God intervene in the debate to crush Job. Indeed, afterwards God declares that Job was speaking the truth about him. It was the other three he disapproved of, and was even angry with (42:7).

However, in one sense, Job is being put in his place, more precisely his true place in creation. He is forcefully reminded that he is less than God and will never understand his ways which are 'too wonderful for me to know' (42:3). But he is still above all else that God has made. He is God's image in the world, the pinnacle of creation. It's as though God is saying, majestic and powerful as these other creatures are, I can't have a relationship with them as I can with you, Job. I can't talk with them as I can with you. So let's talk!

The monsters in this speech are not real characters in the drama. They don't have speaking parts. In reality, they are offstage. But Job is a character with a voice, so he is to use it. Animals can't complain when life goes wrong for them, but humans can, and we are allowed to. God would rather hear from us. He will not get angry over this.

God did not speak in order to destroy Job or punish him further, but to raise him up to be once more the person he was created to be. Job is to stand up and be a man. We might say, he is to 'man up', even when all he has known, enjoyed and loved has collapsed around him. Perhaps the main lesson from all this is that knowing our true place in creation, below God but above the animals, and living on in that knowledge, is more important than having answers to all our questions about life's adversities and wretchedness.

But didn't Job also say, 'I despise myself and repent in dust and ashes' (42:6)? Doesn't this indicate further desolation and self-loathing? If God didn't intend this, then what is Job saying here?

Quoted above is the standard translation of this verse, but this does not match the Hebrew text very well. Nor does it explain what it was that Job felt he needed to repent of.

Translators variously tell us that Job abhors himself, hates himself, detests himself. But this misses the fact that there is no object in the Hebrew text. The word 'myself' is added by translators to make more sense in English, but this skews the meaning. What Job despises is not himself but his previous stance at the end of God's first speech when he decided to 'say no more' (40:5). What he repents of is not any sinfulness or what he said during the debate, but his resolution to remain silent when God had told him to brace himself like a man and answer him (40:7). Now he has heard more from God and seen more of him, Job has changed his mind about his previous decision. This is what he is renouncing or recanting. He will not stay silent now.

However, the word translated 'repent' also requires some comment. Its root is n-h-m, which gives rise to the words for consolation or comfort. We find this earlier in 2:11, where his three friends turn up to comfort him. The same root occurs several times in the book where it is translated as comfort (7:13, 16:2, 21:34, 29:35, 42:11).

And then Job's reference to dust and ashes also needs explaining as misunderstanding can easily occur here. The phrase is used only three times in the Old Testament. Once is earlier in Job when he states, 'I am reduced to dust and ashes' (30:19), but again there is no sense of repentance in this statement. The phrase is not to be confused with sackcloth and ashes, which does refer to extreme repentance and remorse. Rather, it is a recognition of our physical origin and an acceptance of the fragile nature of humanity. It is also an expression of our mortality. Despite being only human Job has been heard by his creator, who wants a dialogue with him. Amazing!

The third mention of the phrase occurs in Genesis 18:27 when Abraham is pleading with God over Sodom and Gomorrah: 'I have been so bold as to speak to the Lord, though I am nothing but dust and ashes.' Again Abraham is not repenting over anything. He is simply recognising his humanity. A mere man talking to God in this way!

Job is expressing himself in the same way. He will talk to God now as he has come to realise that even a creature of dust and ashes may speak to the ruler of the universe and hear from him. If he has learnt nothing else from all his suffering then this is a major lesson in itself.

If we understand 42:6 in these ways outlined above, then we will arrive at a very different conclusion about Job's final response to God. Job now accepts that his initial response to God (I'm going to say nothing from now on) was inadequate and not what God desired, and so he repents of this attitude. He is also now comfortable with his mortality, his 'dust and ashes'. Job's friends have not comforted him but God has. God has taken him seriously. He has appeared to him and shown that he wants a continual conversation with him.

From all this we can see why God's second speech is both necessary and even essential. It also makes God seem less cruel. He is not grinding Job into the dust but getting him back on track after this traumatic experience. At last Job is comforted.

We have tried in this chapter to unpack some of the complexities of a difficult part of the book of Job. Whether successful in this or not, we must now move on. In our final chapter on Job we will provide a summary and some final thoughts on this amazing book.

Chapter Nineteen

Job:
Summary and Conclusions

The book of Job is in a class by itself. With its vivid vocabulary and rich poetry it displays a degree of literary mastery rarely equalled. But these qualities can remain unappreciated as the book as a whole is difficult to digest, especially in one sitting. Perhaps, though, its aim is not to be a quick and easy read but to stimulate thought. Clearly, much careful consideration is needed to be able to grapple with the complexities of the arguments and the interplay between characters.

We have examined the book of Job as a protracted drama set in patriarchal times but with an opening scene in heaven where God is challenged by the 'satan' (the accuser or opposer) that Job only serves God and follows his ways because of the blessings this brings. Remove these and he will turn against God. To prove him wrong, God allows this adversary to take away everything from Job except his life and a story of great agony and suffering has begun.

Job's friends are of very little help in this situation. They uphold the assumption that a person's suffering is in direct proportion to his sin. Their case is simple and, to them, obvious. Calamities such as Job has experienced can only occur to a great sinner. But their arguments are too rigid and so they are unable to handle exceptions to the norm. This is a common mistake, repeated whenever we refuse to consider there may be factors of which we have no notion at all. To be totally unyielding in such circumstances displays a lack of wisdom. We cannot always insist we know what God must surely think and do. God is always free. Knowing him comes from revelation and will never eliminate the mystery of his unknowability. This is one lesson we can take from reading Job and one way we can grow in wisdom.

Even if we regard the format of Job as a drama, we should remember it is still part of the Word of God so we must also assess its theology. Is the book of Job a thesis on the problem of suffering or does it provide a revelation of how God governs this world? Perhaps its intention is to illustrate how God refuses to justify his ways to man? Possibly all these, and more! It can speak to us in many ways.

From Job, we can learn a lot about God that we may otherwise miss. In particular, we cannot insist that he should conform to our views. God alone reveals to us what he is like and defines all things for us. He is not subject to a higher independent set of principles. Rather, principles exist because of who he is and because he made them so.

When we think about the specific issue of suffering our natural minds may take us in many directions. We could see suffering as a form of retribution or as a means of disciplining us or testing us. Maybe we just accept that suffering is in some way inevitable as we are all sinners and that there will always be an element of mystery about it. Or we could assume suffering is random and generally meaningless, with no moral overtones at all. So many ideas could assail our thoughts. One function of the book of Job is to help us assess our thinking in these areas and become wiser in this matter.

One thing that is made clear from the prologue onwards is that innocent suffering *does* exist. Denying this is futile. Nowhere in the book is this contradicted. It is not a viable option for us to always associate suffering with guilt in some way. And even if some suffering may be traced to a particular sin, we should still beware of concluding that it is intended as a punishment. Overall, we should learn to tread wisely in this area.

Another point to emerge from the book of Job is that suffering, however severe, need not exclude or diminish our ability to communicate with God. It may even enhance it. Terrible as his suffering was, Job faced another possible tragedy, namely that in the midst of such adversity he could have stopped believing that anything had meaning any more. But in the final analysis, he avoided two possible extremes, either holding on to a dogmatic orthodoxy that didn't meet his needs, or descending into an escapist form of atheism.

We can certainly conclude from the book of Job that man cannot fully understand the ways of God, even in the most demanding of circumstances. But it is still possible to have a greater revelation of the incomparable majesty and power of God which in itself can be transformational. Even if it doesn't change our circumstances, it can change us. Meeting with God in the midst of trauma and drama can do this. He may not answer the questions which dominate our minds but he can provide the best answer of all, himself.

The book of Job is a supreme example of how our most profound questions of life often have at best partial answers. At most, Job offers approaches to these questions, but ones which should help us think more deeply about the problems raised. Moreover, by refusing to provide us with simplistic responses, this book points beyond itself, into the New Testament, and ultimately to Christ himself.

James realised this when he commended the perseverance of Job. He expects us to have heard about Job and his story, and God's part in it (Jas 5:11). He knows that through this book we will gain a certain amount of wisdom, perhaps even a new type of wisdom. Maybe one without all the answers we seek but one which will enhance our existing knowledge and life experiences.

There is one moment in the gospels which resonates with the story of Job. In Luke 22:31, Jesus tells Peter that Satan has asked to have him in order to sift him as wheat, which presumably refers to a severe testing involving painful experiences. In fact, it seems Satan asked for all the disciples like this, as a correct translation should involve the plural form, 'all of you' or 'each of you'. In this case we learn that Jesus prayed specifically for Peter over this, not in order to prevent it happening but that it would lead to greater faith and service. Jesus is content to allow Peter to be tested like this, but he puts in a counter-plea or prayer that Peter's faith will come through, and that he can then strengthen others. We can trust that Jesus is also holding back all that Satan has for us, and when he does allow us to be tested it will not be beyond what we can bear (cf. 1

Cor. 10:13). We should also notice that when it came to his turn, Jesus did not prevent his own suffering or testing, but for our sake was prepared to go through 'the hour when darkness reigns' (see Luke 22:53). Such hours do exist.

Given the nature of the book it is perhaps not surprising that there are so few quotations from Job in the New Testament. There is also the additional point that, at the end of the book, God declares that the friends 'have not spoken the truth about me' (42:7). So although we continue to read their speeches as part of the overall drama, we should be wary of taking anything they say out of context. Quoting a verse or two from these passages could lead to error of our own. It is the book as a whole that brings us revelation as part of the Word of God. Its theology comes through its totality, not via each individual verse, some of which may simply not be true. Just as in any book or drama what a character says may not reflect the author's own beliefs, so in the case of Job we must beware of taking our theology from isolated comments of certain individuals. It takes wisdom to discern whether what is being spoken in Job truly expresses the mind of God.

One person with such wisdom was Paul who quotes directly from Job twice; once in Romans 11:35, which is taken from God's second speech in Job 41:11, and once in 1 Corinthians 3:19 where he quotes a snippet from Eliphaz's first speech in Job 5:13a. Other than that, New Testament writers steer clear of including excerpts from Job in their own works.

But it would equally be a mistake to assume that everything the three friends said must be wrong. What they express is the kind of traditional deed-outcome wisdom that we find in Proverbs, so it has some validity. But it was not appropriate for Job's situation. It was misapplied, and so created discord and further distress. We have seen previously that such proverbial statements are generally true but are not guaranteed to be so in every situation. Wisdom is needed to decide when they do apply. This is where the three friends fell short. Their form of wisdom had become fossilised. They had made fixed rules out of generalisations, and so were incapable of dealing with the apparent contradictions that life throws up. This does not mean that their views are to be dismissed completely. Their words remain essentially true, but they are not the only words of wisdom.

The debate we find in Job occurs when a particular kind of wisdom hardens into a rigid interpretation of reality as a whole, which then clashes with experience. Thankfully, most of the time our experience agrees with what Proverbs says rather than what Job goes through. Yet from time to time things happen to show there is much in life which cannot be explained by the wisdom of Proverbs.

The book of Job has been variously called 'wisdom in crisis' or 'wisdom in revolt', and is seen as a protest against the dogmatic assertions and trite formulae of proverbial wisdom. But Job is included in the wisdom literature precisely because it differs from Proverbs rather than repeats what we already know. There is room in the Old Testament for several divergent strands of wisdom. You may recall that the Hebrew word for wisdom, *hokmah*, has no plural form, so we can't talk about different wisdoms, but we can refer to different traditions or doctrines of wisdom. The book of Job grants us permission to challenge any particular wisdom tradition if it fails to be appropriate. However, we ought to add that the traditional deed-outcome perspective on life will always remain largely valid. It is just that Job can serve as a counterfoil to it when this seems to let us down. Overall, it would be wrong to say that Job contradicts Proverbs but it does challenge what is offered there if this becomes all in all. Rather its aim is to supplement the book of Proverbs by developing a greater understanding of God, ourselves and life.

As for the very ending of the book of Job with its 'happy ever after' feel-good factor, this is not intended to establish one view of wisdom above all others. Rather it is a recognition that Job has been changed by his meeting with the Almighty. Moreover, the happy ending is still no resolution to the debate or a full compensation for the suffering he went through. It had all still happened. It wasn't a bad dream, and he would have to live with its memory. Moreover, the sons and daughters he had lost were not returned to him. They remained gone from his life. Anyone who has lost a child will know that later children do not take away that pain.

Incidentally, his seven new sons are not named but, unusually in scripture, we are told the names of his three new daughters. Also unusual is that Job grants them an inheritance along with their brothers even though they would presumably marry one day.

One final point. In Job 19:25-26 we read that even in the midst of his anguish, Job could state: 'I know that my redeemer lives, and that in the end he will stand on the earth. And after my skin has been destroyed, yet in my flesh I will see God.' This is one of the better-known parts of Job, though rather complex to study in detail. But it is worth noting that when Job was translated from Hebrew into Greek, in the version known as the Septuagint, an extra verse was added to the end of the final chapter: 'And it is written that Job will rise again with those whom the Lord raises up.' Perhaps in some way, the book of Job helped the Jewish faith to start to look beyond this life to some kind of future restoration and even resurrection.

Overall, this has been a taxing book to explore, and more challenges await us as we turn next to the book of Ecclesiastes.

Chapter Twenty

Ecclesiastes: Meet Your Teacher

We now turn our attention to another book in the biblical wisdom literature, Ecclesiastes. Like Job, this book also reacts against the traditional dogmatic wisdom found in the book of Proverbs whose limitations can, in certain circumstances, lead us into a cul-de-sac. However, Ecclesiastes differs significantly from Job in several ways. It examines the big questions of life from the viewpoint of an observer rather than a victim, from the perspective of doubt rather than suffering, and from a consideration of having everything you could possibly want rather than losing everything you once had.

Ecclesiastes is a strange book, relatively easy to understand but more difficult to come to terms with. Its mood is largely one of cynicism and pessimism; its message full of fatalism and futility. It can leave us wondering whether we have to agree with all it contains or even how it got into our Bible in the first place. We may also ask how often we ought to turn to its pages and how reading it is meant to inspire us.

It may be surprising to learn that whereas within the Jewish faith, Job hardly gets a public hearing at all, Ecclesiastes has an annual outing. It is read every year during the autumn Feast of Tabernacles, which is known as a season of rejoicing. It may seem odd to read such a book at a time of great joy but perhaps this is to serve as a reminder that there is another side to life, one which requires deeper thought.

As for its place within the Bible, Ecclesiastes also had an uncertain existence within the Jewish scriptures right up until the end of the first century AD. Its inclusion was contested by some rabbinic schools who rejected it as incoherent, even heretical. Others argued for its acceptance on the grounds of the quality of its internal debate on important religious issues. Eventually, at the Council of Jamnia in AD 90, the school of Hillel prevailed and Ecclesiastes became established within the Ketuvim, or Writings section, of their scriptures. One fact which probably helped quieten doubts about the book's inclusion was the rabbinic tradition that attributed it to Solomon. But was he actually its author?

The Jewish tradition that credits the book to Solomon is simply that, tradition. Today, very few scholars defend this view. Indeed it is very difficult, if not impossible, to justify his authorship, even though it remains a common supposition within many Christian circles.

There are certain clues that have led people towards Solomon as author but these are at best inconclusive and tend to point in a different direction entirely. The opening reference to a 'son of David, king of Jerusalem' (1:1) may hint at Solomon but it is noticeable that he is not named as such here or indeed anywhere else in the rest of the book. Moreover, any idea that this is Solomon is undermined very quickly by his own words. For instance, in 1:12, he says he *was* king over Israel in Jerusalem. Solomon could never say this of himself, that he *had been* king. For instance, he never abdicated. In fact, he was still king when he died.

Then in 1:16 he boasts he was wiser than *anyone* who had ruled over Jerusalem before him. But only one person, David, had preceded him on the throne of Jerusalem, so for Solomon to say he was wiser than *all* who had reigned before him makes little sense. Moreover, he does not claim the full extent of wisdom that was attributed to Solomon in 1 Kings 4:29-31, whose wisdom was greater than all the people of the east or of Egypt. Our author simply says he was wiser than any previous king, rather than wiser than anyone else at all.

Perhaps the most conclusive evidence against claims that Solomon wrote Ecclesiastes is that the vocabulary and style of the Hebrew language used in that book reflects a much later period in Israel's history than the time of Solomon's reign (tenth century BC). For instance, the text includes Persian loanwords that did not appear in the Hebrew language until after the exile. Experts fully agree on a later date, some even suggest as late as the third century BC, possibly between 250 and 200 BC. Certainly the nature of the Hebrew language used in Ecclesiastes does not match that of the proverbs attributed to Solomon, nor is it typical of the time of the early monarchy or indeed of any period leading up to the exile. If Solomon was the author of Ecclesiastes we would have to conclude that the Hebrew language has no consistent history, unless Solomon had access to a time machine, or his wisdom was very far-seeing.

So given all this, we can safely abandon any assertion that Solomon wrote Ecclesiastes, as indeed the author himself seems to do. His reference to himself as a king does not persist throughout the book. In fact, it disappears after chapter 2, when he starts to write from a different standpoint. By the end, in 12:9, he has simply reverted to his opening title of 'the Teacher', someone who is looking to impart knowledge and wisdom to those who will hear him. We will consider this title in detail in a few moments.

Meanwhile, we should point out that this debate about who wrote Ecclesiastes and the conclusion that it was not Solomon, should not trouble us one bit. The ancient world was not as concerned about authorship as we are today with our strict rules. Many works were produced anonymously or under a pseudonym, meaning they were written under a false name. This was not based upon any intention to deceive or be fraudulent. In particular it was quite customary to associate anything relating to wisdom with Solomon. We saw in an earlier chapter how this may have been the case with certain proverbs, and we will meet it again in chapter 26 regarding the apocryphal book The Wisdom of Solomon, which he most definitely could not have written.

So here, in Ecclesiastes, is a literary device to gain our attention. The adoption of a persona (that is, acting or speaking as though you were someone else) was a common way to attract interest. Solomon served as a model of the kind of life the author wanted to evaluate. Here was someone regarded as the wisest man who ever lived and who was also fabulously wealthy, powerful and privileged. He had it all. So what would he conclude about life? Was it all worthwhile?

A piece of writing of this kind has been called a 'royal testament' in that it impersonates a kingly figure with the aim of testing out a particular understanding of reality under the most favourable of circumstances. In this case, the author of Ecclesiastes has put himself in Solomon's shoes and invites us to join him there. He is suggesting we should use our imagination and pretend to be king. And not just any king! Solomon, no less!

Here is a skilful teacher at work, employing the technique of role play to earth his debate in an historical figure, and thus give weight to his arguments and in particular to his conclusion. If a life free of all the usual limitations experienced by mortal men remains empty and meaningless, then this must be true of life as a whole.

Once we have appreciated the book in this particular way we can see why there are several hints in it that might steer us towards Solomon as author but also why there are many indications that this cannot be so. This also explains why the author drops this fictional persona later in the book once it has fulfilled its purpose.

So who is the real author? Can we learn anything about him? We have already mentioned that he calls himself 'the Teacher' at the very beginning of the book and also again at the end. So let's turn to that now and consider what this might mean.

When reading the opening sentence it is easy to focus on the phrases 'son of David, king of Jerusalem', but the key word in 1:1 is 'Teacher'. In Hebrew this is *kohelet*, which when transliterated into English letters is usually written as Qoheleth. That is what we will call him from now on. It is also the title of the book in the Hebrew Scriptures, though we will still refer to this as Ecclesiastes to avoid confusing the author with his book.

The Hebrew word *kohelet* occurs seven times throughout the book: three times in chapter 1 (verses 1, 2 and 12), once in 7:27, and three times in chapter 12 (verses 8, 9 and 10). The question is whether this word is a proper name or just a noun, in this case an occupational title. In one of these verses, 12:8, the definite article also appears. We find *ha-kohelet*, or '*the* Teacher'. Here it seems we are to take it as a title, in particular that of an official post or function. Rather strangely the definite article also occurs in 7:27 but only in the Greek Septuagint (LXX) version of the Hebrew text. It is not clear why it was added in this case. All the other times the word occurs it can operate as a proper name though it remains possible to read it either way.

In technical terms the form of the word *kohelet* is that of the active participle with a feminine ending and is derived from the verbal root q-h-l, which means 'to gather, assemble or collect together'. From this comes the noun *qahal*, which means 'an assembly or congregation' and so can refer to a group of students who have been gathered together to receive instruction. In which case the Qoheleth is the one who has assembled them for this purpose and who then leads them, either in instruction or in debate. Some translations use 'leader of the assembly' as an alternative in the footnote.

Another idea is that the Qoheleth is like the speaker in Parliament or the president of a debating society, someone who oversees others who are participating in a discussion. In this case, the topic for debate would be, is life worth living? Is there any purpose in life?

Some think his role is not restricted to gathering together people in order to instruct them but that it also refers to the way he collected or 'gathered up' proverbs and wise sayings. This makes sense in the light of 12:9-11. Then there is also the strange expression in 7:27 of the Teacher 'adding one thing to another to discover the scheme of things', or more literally 'counting one thing to another to find out the sum'. Here, it seems, is someone who gathers lots of individual facts and opinions in order to find the total meaning and overall truth of a matter.

We said earlier that the Hebrew title of the book in their scriptures is also Qoheleth, so why do we call it Ecclesiastes? Typically with books of the Bible, we have taken up the Greek version of their names. The Greek equivalent of the Hebrew word *qahal* is *ekklesia*, which we are familiar with through words like ecclesiastical. So in the Greek Septuagint (LXX) version of the book, 'Qoheleth' becomes 'the Ecclesiast'. However, we must be clear that there is nothing ecclesiastical about him in our modern terms. He is not a churchman, nor is he a preacher in the way we think of such people today. What we can say about him is that he was a celebrated teacher, a diligent scholar and a skilled writer. He has gained much experience of life and his concern is to pass that on to a younger generation.

We end this chapter by asking whether the book of Ecclesiastes has any discernible structure to help our reading of it. Clearly there is no overall plot or narrative, nor does the book consist of a series of conversations (like Job) or a collection of sayings (like Proverbs). It is more like a notebook, full of reflections and musings. The writer seems to wander about, often repeating himself or at least offering variations on certain recurrent themes. We shall consider some of these later, but for now we can say that the book broadly divides into two sections, chapters 1 to 6 and chapters 7 to 12. However, we can do slightly better than this.

After the opening statement in 1:1 we have an introductory poem (1:2-11), which acts as a preface to the rest of the first half of the book from 1:12 to 6:9. We then have the second half from 6:10 to 11:6 (though some would say that 6:10-12 acts as a preface to this second portion), which is then rounded off by a concluding poem from 11:7 to 12:8. This is then followed by a brief finale (12:9-14), which tells us more about our teacher and what he regards as 'the conclusion of the matter' (12:13).

Beyond this basic outline there is little agreement on how the book is structured. There are some headings and groupings which may help, and there are certain refrains which mark off smaller units within the two main sections. For instance, the first half constantly refers to 'emptiness' and a 'chasing after the wind', while the second employs phrases such as 'who can find out' or 'who knows', implying that such knowledge is elusive at best, or non-existent at worst. There are also other transition markers in the text, such as 'then I turned and saw', 'I gave myself up to' and 'I applied my mind'. Finally, on the matter of structure, we note how his initial statement in 1:2, 'Meaningless! Meaningless! Everything is meaningless!' is repeated at the end in 12:8, thus forming an inclusio, a technical literary device which acts like brackets, holding the whole piece together. Here in these few words is his motto text for his entire thesis, a succinct summation upon which he will expand throughout his work.

In the end it does not matter too much who Qoheleth actually was. Today we meet him only through his writing, so that is how we are to know him. Clearly, he was a wise man who reflected a lot about the life he has known and asked the big questions. The problem for us lies with his answers. Are they just his conclusions or are they to be regarded as truth? Is this God speaking through him?

He is certainly commended for being good at what he does. He was dedicated to his task and worth listening to, if only because he made people think. His words, or at least those sayings he collected and passed on, were like goads (12:9), probing and prodding young minds, provoking them to examine their assumptions and forcing them to rethink. He was both mentor and tormentor.

In our next chapter we will begin to examine some of his words and see how they might goad us in similar ways.

Chapter Twenty-One

Ecclesiastes: Words of the Teacher

So far we have established that while the author of Ecclesiastes may have briefly adopted the persona of Solomon in order to examine whether life would be worthwhile if granted all the privileges of immense wealth, supreme power and unlimited opportunities, overall he identified himself primarily through the Hebrew title of Qoheleth, or Teacher. This is how we will refer to him from now on. But what exactly did this Teacher teach?

Qoheleth wants to take us on an intellectual and spiritual journey to discover the purpose of life and whether in the end it is worth living. We cannot provide a full commentary on all that he says, but we will examine the main points, starting with his well-known opening statement: 'Meaningless! Meaningless! Everything is meaningless.'

Here Qoheleth announces in advance a summary of the results of his search. This is an unusual way to start, dashing our hopes of any kind of positive outcome from the outset. Our expectation is dampened to the point of being drowned. But perhaps this is a tactic on his part, intended not only to alert us to the bad news to come but also to intrigue us into how he reached this totally negative conclusion about life and everything in it. We want to read on!

Some translations of this verse (1:2), such as the Authorised Version and even the New King James Version, use the word 'vanity' as the author hammers out his verdict in stirring fashion: '"Vanity of vanities," says the Preacher, "Vanity of vanities, all is vanity."'

His dramatic use of repetition certainly makes the point, and indeed accurately reflects the Hebrew of this verse. In particular, a phrase of the pattern 'X of X', such as 'Vanity of vanities', is how the Hebrew language indicates the superlative form, in the way that Holy of Holies means the holiest place, and Lord of Lords means the highest Lord. However, we need to be clear that here 'vanity' does not refer to pride or being vain, rather it means 'in vain' or 'futile', hence the correct newer translation of 'meaningless'. Words such as 'futility' or 'emptiness' would also be accurate.

The actual Hebrew word in this verse (1:2) is *hebel*, which means a vapour or breath or anything without real substance. It also indicates something which comes and goes quickly. It is the thinnest of vapours; it is as fleeting as a single breath. Interestingly, this word is behind the name Abel, who certainly had only a relatively brief time on earth compared to others of that pre-flood era.

The word *hebel* is used over thirty times in Ecclesiastes (some say as many as thirty-eight times). It refers to something real and recognisable but which lacks substance or permanence. In general, the Hebrew language prefers concrete metaphors rather than abstract expressions and here the imagery of a vapour or breath works well. Another pertinent image would be that of a soap bubble, which looks pretty for a while but is basically empty and will suddenly vanish leaving nothing behind. Like a soap bubble, life too can abruptly go 'pop'. Even if, like Solomon, you were born with all the privileges life can offer, or if you worked hard to gain many advantages, or even if you won the lottery, life would still be a soap bubble. Maybe a larger, prettier soap bubble, but a soap bubble nonetheless.

This is Qoheleth's conclusion. Even after his 'thought experiment' of a life so wonderful in every way that it would only be possible for an absolute monarch like Solomon, he has found no reason to deny the apparent futility of human existence in general. All we do and hope for is ultimately transient and without gain. The Hebrew word for 'gain' is *yithron*, which also means 'profit' or 'advantage'. It occurs first in 1:3 and again in 2:11, which is a good summary of what Qoheleth has discovered so far. 'Yet when I surveyed all that my hands had done and what I toiled to achieve, everything was meaningless, a chasing after the wind; nothing was gained under the sun.'

It is no surprise that Qoheleth often links his use of the word *hebel* (meaningless) with the phrase 'a chasing after the wind', another metaphor for a life full of activity but ultimately of no lasting gain. As well as in 2:11 quoted above, this pairing occurs several more times (see, for instance, 1:14, 2:17, 2:26, 4:4, 4:16, 6:9).

Overall, Qoheleth stresses the impermanence of all things, the inescapability of death, the injustices of life, and the likely lack of value in working hard. No wonder we find the book depressing. But we cannot fault Qoheleth's determination and efforts in his pursuit for meaning. His search is widespread and his focus is one of firm resolve. In 1:13 he declares, 'I applied my mind to study and to explore by wisdom all that is done under the heavens.'

Two different verbs are used here. The word for study is based upon *darash*, which indicates a diligent and thorough investigation, one which involves digging as deep as necessary to get at the truth. The other verb, *tur*, translated as 'explore', also suggests that extraordinary measures are being taken, similar to that of an undercover agent spying on anyone and anything relevant to his mission. Taken together, these verbs suggest Qoheleth left no stone unturned in his relentless quest for reality. This is summarised in 7:25, where he states, 'So I turned my mind to understand, to investigate and to search out wisdom and the scheme of things . . .'

But what about his conclusions? Is our world really characterised by superficiality, transience and worthlessness? What becomes clear as we read through his book is that his investigation is hampered by two considerable constraints. These are indicated by two phrases which Qoheleth employs repeatedly. One is 'under the sun', which by some counts occurs twenty-eight times in this book but nowhere else in the Bible. The other is 'all the days of my life'. But what do these mean, and especially what do they imply about his search?

'Under the sun' is a way of saying 'everywhere the suns shines its light' and refers to this physical world, what we can see around us. Qoheleth can observe all the natural phenomena but he cannot see beyond the horizon of the material world into a spiritual dimension. His other repeated phrase, 'All the days of my life', means 'while I am still alive', suggesting that Qoheleth can say nothing about what might happen after death.

Through these two phrases, Qoheleth is admitting that his search for meaning is limited to the here and now, to this world and this life. He cannot see beyond these to the next life or the world to come. Being thus hemmed in, he is inevitably forced to conclude that everything is meaningless. True, we may find a certain satisfaction at times through our work, what we do and enjoy, but we are not to expect any lasting answers regarding the purpose of it all. In particular, he is telling us that a life lived only for what this world offers must result in pessimism and produce absurdities beyond our comprehension.

In our exploration of biblical wisdom we have often met the question: 'What is true wisdom and where can it be found?' The answer, we have discovered, lies with God himself. Only he can provide this and we need to ask him for it, which means looking beyond our natural world and towards heaven and eternity. What we find in these Old Testament wisdom books is a preparation for what will eventually be revealed in the New Testament, and also regarding Christ himself, who as the wisdom of God came into our world from beyond our own existence in time and space. Meanwhile, all Qoheleth can do is highlight the feelings of frustration and futility about life which are common to all humanity, and show us that the reason for this is a narrow view of life which leaves God out of it. To this end, Qoheleth employs a variety of literary techniques and forms, some of which we will investigate next.

In 1:3-11 there is a wonderfully expressive poem on the patterns found in nature. Qoheleth observes how the sun, the wind and the natural water courses are all in constant motion yet end up going nowhere. They move in endless cycles but nothing changes. What goes around, comes around. Qoheleth uses these self-evident and undeniable characteristics of the natural world to illustrate his claim that the same is true for human life. Generations come and go in endless succession, engaging in an outpouring of energy and effort, but for what profit? Life is like a merry-go-round. We get on and enjoy the ride for a while but who knows for how long? We may go round and round several times, only to get off at precisely the same place we got on with nothing to show for it. His famous statement in 1:9, that there is nothing new under the sun, may not be factually or historically true, but it does indicate a sense of world-weariness, how a daily routine of toil may feel over the course of a lifetime.

A second poem occurs in 3:1-8, and is one of the better-known parts of the book with its recitation of a time for this and a time for that. But what is it telling us?

This poem has been read in several different ways. Some see a dark side to it. Here is the tyranny of time in which nothing good lasts for long before it is replaced. Above all, it shows we are not the masters of our own lives. We cannot control when things happen or say why they happen when they do. Our lives are dominated by uncertainty and we can only submit to these seasonal whims.

Others prefer the more pleasant idea of the poem depicting the tapestry of time, with all its variety, making up the full picture of life. Still others refer to it as the tide of time, with its 'to and fro' between opposites reflecting the ebb and flow of life.

But perhaps best of all is to regard it as a wisdom poem. We have seen previously that wisdom is about making the right choices at the right time, which involves recognising which 'time' or 'season' we are now in. We need to know that our 'times' are not chaotic, or uncontrolled. God appoints them. But rather than be fatalistic or resigned we should be alert to the time he has currently given to us. This is wisdom at work. We can't choose these times for ourselves, but we can be ready for them and act accordingly within what God sends. For instance, we cannot expect to be joyful at all times, but we should make sure we do not miss out on joy when its time comes. We have also seen how the wisdom tradition highlights the value of knowing when to say something, and when to be silent. Overall, we cannot dictate the times but we can respond wisely to them.

In 3:11 we find a summary of this poem, namely that God has made everything beautiful in its own time. But the rest of this verse is difficult to translate. There are many alternatives, often placed in the footnotes. The problem word is *ha'olam*, whose primary meaning refers to something which is hidden but which will also endure into the unknown future, hence translations may use either the word 'mystery' or 'eternity'. So the verse might be saying that man is aware that this flow of various 'times' continues forever by God's appointment (the eternal aspect), or it might be indicating that the precise reason behind what happens, and when, is hidden from man due to our inability to comprehend the eternal (the mystery aspect). However hard we try to discover what determines this tide of events, it will always remain unknown to us.

Chapter 3 ends with a strange little passage in verses 19-21. Qoheleth sees that death is inevitable but this presents him with an unresolved dilemma. He knows from Genesis that we are in some way 'like the animals' and that, like them, we return to dust after death. But his two constraints of this world and this life means he is unclear as to what happens next. Like the animals, one day we will stop breathing. In that sense, their death and ours look similar. But then what? What happens to our spirit? Is our ultimate end different from theirs? At this point, Qoheleth can tell us no more. We need a greater revelation than he can provide. We need an even greater teacher.

Meanwhile, in our next chapter, we will examine some more of the words of this teacher.

Chapter Twenty-Two

Ecclesiastes: More Words of the Teacher

We noted previously that Qoheleth operated under two constraints. He could not see beyond this world or this life. Nevertheless, he still had many worthwhile things to say within the wisdom tradition of his time, so we will continue to look through some of these, picking up from where we left off last time, starting with chapter 4.

The next few chapters cover many topics with seemingly no clear structure in mind. At times it reads more like a notebook, a series of jottings or musings, in which Qoheleth intersperses his own personal observations with sayings or proverbial statements which he had collected in order to illustrate his main points. We are told about this later in 12:9 where we read that the Teacher 'pondered and searched out and set in order many proverbs'.

The opening of chapter 4 is especially gloomy. What particularly disturbs Qoheleth is the amount of oppression and injustice in the world. This leads him to some grim conclusions. In verse 2 he states it is better to be dead than alive. But worse follows in verse 3 when he declares that even better than this is to have never been born, something which we have come across previously when Job gave voice to the depths of his despair in Job chapter 3.

Chapter 5 takes us into the Temple with advice on how to guard our steps and our tongue, otherwise our time in God's presence could be as meaningless as our life elsewhere. Many sayings then follow on the theme of money and our desire to accumulate as much as possible for ourselves. The key verses are those which contain a reference to God where we are repeatedly told that all our wealth is to be regarded as a gift from God, along with life itself (5:18–6:2).

We mentioned earlier that many commentators suggest the book divides into two parts somewhere around the end of chapter 6. Certainly, in chapter 7 we meet a different approach as Qoheleth speaks to us almost exclusively through proverbial sayings. He is now being more insistent on certain things rather than offering personal reflections. He starts with a section on wisdom in which the key word is 'better', which occurs eight times in the first ten verses.

We are immediately confronted with a rather startling statement. In the second half of verse 1 we are told that the day of our death is better than the day we were born. His follow-up remark, in verse 2, is that it is therefore better to attend a funeral than a birthday party. His point is that we need to be reminded of the inevitability of our own death. We don't have a date for this (unlike our birthday) so we need something to make us think ahead to when this might happen. To be aware of the ticking clock is good for us. Death has more to teach us than birth. Parties don't make us think in the way that funerals do. At which of these are you most likely to pray?

Qoheleth is also at this point exploring the depressing fact that when you are gone from this world, everything you had then belongs to someone else, and you've no idea what will happen to it next (6:12). But he does have one positive suggestion to make. 'A good name is better than fine perfume' (7:1a). The one thing you do leave behind that doesn't get passed on to someone else is your reputation. We all want to make a good impression on others. That's why people buy expensive perfume (or aftershave!). This is the quick way to be noticed! Gaining a good name or reputation takes longer, but ultimately is better. How do we want to be remembered? Perhaps that's another reason why attending a funeral is beneficial. It makes us think, what will people say about us when we are no longer here?

All these 'better' proverbs stress that wisdom is living for the future rather than the present. It involves looking ahead. The wise man takes the long view. The fool lives only for the day.

From 7:11 onwards we have an evaluation of wisdom, its pros and cons. On the positive side, it provides greater security than any amount of inherited money (v11-12) and makes you more powerful than those who govern a whole city (v19). Yet human wisdom also has its limitations. It cannot tell you what will happen in the future let alone guarantee that it will go your way. Only God knows the future; he is sovereign over all things (v13-14).

In verses 23-24 we find the same questions we have repeatedly come across regarding wisdom. Where is wisdom to be found? Who can discover it? Qoheleth has shown great determination to be as wise as possible.

He has found out as much as he can but, ultimately, he is forced to accept his limitations in this respect. Most of the time wisdom remains far off. It is profound, even unfathomable at times.

In verse 26 Qoheleth issues a similar warning to one we have met before in Proverbs. Beware the woman who can lead you astray! Many traps await the foolish young man. As we have seen, wisdom is necessary when forming such relationships, especially when looking for a life partner. But it seems here that Qoheleth has a very negative attitude towards women, especially in verse 28, where he claims not to have found even one upright woman among a thousand. But then his view of men isn't much better, just one in a thousand, a difference of 0.1 per cent. Perhaps he regards himself as that special 'one in a thousand'! What we need to realise in these verses is that Qoheleth is reporting his own personal experience rather than giving us an absolute truth. Verse 29, however, can be taken more dogmatically when he states that God made mankind to be upright but we've all gone our own way, seeking our own schemes, thus making life intolerable at times.

In chapter 8, Qoheleth is again trying to bring some wisdom into difficult situations. For instance, those in positions of authority may abuse their power and do what they please, but overall it remains wise to be obedient and not to argue. He knows that fearing God means things work out better, though he isn't always sure how. Once again, Qoheleth is limited by his inability to see anything that might occur after death by way of rewards and punishments. But one issue he can understand is that if crime is not punished at once then it encourages others to do wrong; justice should be swift and seen to be so, a point that patently remains true in all societies today (v11).

In 9:1-10 there is another cheerless passage reminding us that in the end we all join the dead. There is a common destiny for all, however we have lived. So what's the point? Just enjoy life now the best you can within your meaningless existence. Judaism at that time had no clear perception of life after death. You just 'slept with your fathers' (meaning ancestors) but there was no thought of waking again. Sheol (Hades in Greek) was a vague, shadowy place for departed spirits who did nothing. They were just waiting. But for what? It was like being in a station waiting room but with no sign of any trains coming. Some form of belief in an afterlife developed among the Jews when in exile, and by the time of Jesus this was more prevalent, though the Sadducees continued to deny any possibility of resurrection.

Qoheleth is trying to affirm life as best he can. Where there's life there's hope, he seems to be saying (9:4). He asserts that a live dog is better than a dead lion. In those days, dogs were not kept as pets but were wild creatures, often despised, whereas a lion was regarded as the finest of all the beasts. Basically, Qoheleth is saying that any kind of life is better than being dead, which seems to contradict his earlier statements in 4:2-3 that the dead are happier than the living, and that even better was to have never been born at all. Perhaps thinking so much about death is leaving him rather confused. Or perhaps, like any good teacher, he is offering another perspective for us to consider. Certainly he is telling us to enjoy life while we can before we end up in the realm of the dead, where he reckons there is nothing to look forward to, nothing to do. Nor is there any chance of finding wisdom there either (9:10).

In 9:11 we find a saying that is well known to us today ('The race is not to the swift or the battle to the strong'), and some parts of chapter 10 have also given rise to familiar sayings today. For instance in verse 1, 'a fly in the ointment', and in verse 20, 'a little bird told me'.

As we have come to expect from proverbial statements in general, those in Ecclesiastes are shrewd, often witty, and contain turns of phrase which can pack a punch. As before, these maxims provide nuggets of wisdom to help us get through life with greater success.

Chapter 11 opens with what seems to be some advice on trade and commerce. In verse 1, translators have come up with many interesting variations on 'cast your bread upon the waters and you will find it again after many days', suggesting that this is primarily about making foreign investments. 'Bread' becomes 'money' and 'upon the waters' suggests 'overseas', with 'find it again' indicating you will get a good return or make a substantial profit. In fact, the basis of the saying is more along the lines that generosity will be repaid one day. As for verse 2, this is the equivalent of 'don't put all your eggs in one basket', which is good advice financially as well as in many other ways.

From 11:7 onwards we get an extended passage on the problems of getting old, with 12:1-7 being one of the best-known parts of the whole book. The phrase 'light is sweet' (11:7) tells us that each day is a precious gift. As you wake each morning and the darkness of sleep gives way to the sunlight of the morning, take time to give thanks. Take nothing for granted. Qoheleth contrasts the light of being alive with the darkness of being dead, adding the gloomy but valid reminder that however long you live you'll be dead much longer!

Being young is a joy and can be a time of great happiness, but it is also a time to remember the one who created you and gave you this life, something which is largely ignored or even denied these days. In particular, during your youthful vigour, realise that the clock is ticking and old age is coming. Typically, Qoheleth's advice is to enjoy your youth as one day you will look back and it will all seem meaningless.

Chapter 12 verses 1-7 provide us with a vivid, yet poignant, description of old age. Here is a graphic portrayal of the body as it ages. Various images are used to depict physical decline. Muscles start to weaken and teeth drop out. Eyes and ears lose their powers, sights and sounds grow dim. Sleep can be elusive, especially as dawn breaks. Certain fears take hold, such as falling or being jostled in a crowd. Spending time outside is more troublesome as life generally becomes slower and more unsteady. The almond blossom represents white hair, and the once sprightly grasshopper can now hardly move as the spring in our step has gone forever. Sexual desire dwindles; indeed it is increasingly difficult to find the desire to do anything much at all. Overall, there is an increasing sense of desolation as faculties are lost, old friends die and hopes have to be abandoned.

The final scene, in verses 6-7, describes death itself, depicted as a derelict well, no longer able to supply life-giving water. At the end of life there is nothing to show but an empty well and a smashed jar. Qoheleth does suggest that our spirit returns to God, but then what?

In general, the young don't think that they will become old. At that age it is easy to see older people as having always been old, even born that way! But one day it dawns on us that this is our journey too. This can be a profitable moment, making us stop and think that life is short and temporary.

The final part of Ecclesiastes (12:9-14) resembles an epilogue, which is generally regarded as having been written by someone else, perhaps one of his students, rather than by Qoheleth himself. It is *about* him, rather than *by* him. The motto theme of meaninglessness in 12:8 would be a fitting final statement from Qoheleth, reflecting how he started in 1:2. So most likely what we have here at the very end is an appendage which serves to commend and approve the work of the Teacher.

The use of 'my son' in 12:12, although common in Proverbs, is not found elsewhere in Ecclesiastes, again suggesting these final verses come from a different hand. Otherwise the content of the epilogue is consistent with the rest of the book, with the final two verses summing up the fundamental lesson that Qoheleth gained from his quest and which he passed on to others.

There is one more point to be drawn from this ending. Qoheleth collected proverbs, which in itself is a good thing, but there is a warning attached, almost a health warning. Once you start collecting proverbs you will find there is no limit. They will fill volume upon volume. This will be overwhelming, and will wear you out. And if there was no end to the making of books then, how much more so now! We could also add that today there is no end to the creating of websites and too much surfing can cause exhaustion! Basically, the point here is that it is impossible to absorb all the so-called wisdom of the past, which is mostly human ideas and opinions anyway. Sorting through it all would be confusing and time-consuming. Asking God for wisdom when you need it, is by far the best option.

For Qoheleth, all he had enjoyed in life passed into insignificance once he started looking back. He realised this can be how we all feel in later life, as the years take their toll. So enjoy life and appreciate it while you can, otherwise you will live in total frustration. But he is also wise enough to realise that such frustration can be positive, inviting us to search for more wisdom.

In our next chapter we will draw our section on Ecclesiastes to a close with some concluding thoughts on the book as a whole.

Chapter Twenty-Three

Ecclesiastes: Some Final Thoughts

We will round off our consideration of the book of Ecclesiastes by drawing together some final thoughts and trying to answer certain questions.

One of these is why Ecclesiastes is in the Bible at all, given that its negativism and pessimism seem to be at odds with the rest of the canon. At first sight, it is certainly curious that both Judaism and Christianity considered this book to be worthy of a place in their scriptures as in many ways it seems alien. Jewish sages did debate whether or not to include it, but in the end it was accepted for its contribution towards a religious debate that was seen as necessary and important. As with all canonical books, the test for inclusion was that it had been approved within the religious life of the believing community. Only then was a book officially declared as sacred and authoritative. Or to put it slightly differently, as Paul did to Timothy, it had to be 'useful for teaching, rebuking, correcting and training in righteousness' (2 Tim. 3:16). But this simply begs the next question: how can Ecclesiastes be useful? We'll attempt to answer this now.

There is certainly a daring originality about the book of Ecclesiastes. Here is an exceptional voice within the Old Testament, one that can easily be dismissed as marginal. Moreover, if Qoheleth's pessimism was all that the book offered then there might be something harmful about it. But although Ecclesiastes may reside at the border of orthodoxy, it remains a crucial step away from heresy or unbelief.

This is a key point. Qoheleth is no atheist or even agnostic doubter. He affirms Israel's faith in Yahweh as a fundamental presupposition of his writing and teaching. His theme of meaninglessness is not the same as outright nihilism which is atheistic. His cry is different. God exists but he remains mysterious and so much about his dealings with men cannot be known. Qoheleth is puzzled by the absurdities of life yet he is convinced of the need for faith in God. It could be argued that his faith is rather minimal, less than that usually found among the Jewish people in the past. But his scepticism won't descend into atheism. He knows God is there and believes everything is under his control. As such he can affirm life in God's world. He will not descend into the folly of saying in his heart, 'There is no God.'

Qoheleth recognises the tensions of life and its experiences. He battles with profound paradoxes and faces genuine mental struggles. He is torn between what he cannot help seeing and what he still cannot help believing. He observes an inherent frustration about life as a whole, but his faith tells him there is a reason, even though he will not find it 'under the sun' or during 'all the days of his life'.

Another question concerns the role of the book of Ecclesiastes within the wisdom tradition as a whole. Does

Ecclesiastes sit within this tradition or stand opposed to it? In the next chapter we will examine the relationship between the three wisdom books – Proverbs, Job and Ecclesiastes – but for now we can comment that, as is typical of the wisdom literature in general, Qoheleth is seeking answers to the familiar questions of what is wisdom and where can it be found.

Qoheleth is as motivated as anyone can be in his search within all possible observable data for an understanding of human experience. As such he stands within the wisdom tradition, even if at times he is rather ambivalent towards traditional wisdom and challenges its value. His teaching is more likely to end with a question mark than a confident exclamation mark but, even so, he is rightly called wise for the reasons given towards the end of his book (12:9-11). His special ability was to be able to engage others in debate, and this is how we should understand what he has produced. Here is an internal debate within the Hebrew faith, and indeed within the Judeo-Christian tradition as a whole. If he provides a more discordant note than others, this is because the key has already been established.

But there is another intriguing question about Qoheleth which bears some consideration. Did he personally believe everything he said and wrote, or was he merely raising questions for others to debate? In other words, was he teaching out of personal conviction or was he simply presenting his pupils with a series of scenarios to guide them into thinking for themselves? If the latter, then perhaps to that end he chose to employ another tactic. As well as assuming the persona of King Solomon to add weight to his arguments, he may also have taken on the role of a pessimist or sceptic. By presenting the viewpoints and reasoning of such people, Qoheleth's intention was to stir his pupils (and us, his readers) into asking questions about the implications of such beliefs and where they ultimately lead. He is also challenging us to ask ourselves if this is what we really want to believe about life. As a gifted teacher Qoheleth would have been more than capable of identifying with those he didn't necessarily agree with. He could talk their language and argue their case, and then skilfully display the consequences of such beliefs, perhaps even to the extent of turning people away from following such negative attitudes. It may be that what we have here is Qoheleth meeting the secularist or cynic on his own terms in order to demonstrate the emptiness of their position.

Reading Ecclesiastes in this way (and it is only one suggestion), means we can see it not so much as Qoheleth's own final textbook on such matters but more like a collection of notes and ideas that he had gathered in order to 'goad his pupils'. We said earlier that the book gave the impression of being more like a notebook than a carefully constructed thesis. Here, perhaps, is a compendium of the material he used for such didactic purposes.

Although this may not be a common way of looking at Ecclesiastes, it does have certain advantages. Firstly, the book acquires a stronger justification for its place within the inspired Word of God, one which perhaps we can accept more readily. Alongside this, the book takes on a greater significance and purpose for us today in our increasingly secular and cynical society. We live in a world full of pessimism and unbelief, dominated by existentialist ideology and run by human wisdom which is constrained by the things of this world and this life.

One of the challenges for Christians in the modern world is to find meeting points with those for whom despair, disappointment and doubt are commonplace. Before we can engage effectively with unbelievers we need to understand how they think and feel, and the issues they face. Ecclesiastes can help us here. It strikes a chord with those who find belief difficult. In particular, it reflects where people are without Christ. Unknowingly, Qoheleth has provided us with a work of Christian apologetics, something to aid our pre-evangelism. For many, this book could be a persuasive preparation for the gospel message, a step on the way to faith in Christ.

For this reason, if for no other, Ecclesiastes remains an essential book for Christians to understand. It is as important as ever to appreciate the continuing value of its message, especially how it points to the need for a greater wisdom, for a greater than Solomon (see Luke 11:31), for someone to bring us wisdom from beyond this world and this life. The New Testament resolves many of the questions posed by Qoheleth because it demonstrates that Christ came to us as the wisdom of God (1 Cor. 1:24) and that he continues to be so because of his resurrection. He now lives beyond this life. He didn't just provide better answers. He is the answer, the answer to all futility and frustration, to cynicism and vexation of spirit.

In addition to portraying Christ in this way, the New Testament continues to press home some of the main themes of Ecclesiastes, to demonstrate how meaningless life is without God at the centre. Perhaps the most striking passage is in Romans 8:19-23, where Paul describes how, by God's will, the whole of creation in its current state has been subjected to frustration and bondage. Like us, it needs to be liberated and redeemed. Meanwhile, creation, also like us, is groaning at what it experiences. This explains why life is so painful at times and why we can never find total fulfilment in this world alone. God simply does not allow this. He is forcing us to look beyond what we currently enjoy. But, at the same time, the message of the New Testament reveals that God's plan of redemption includes a new heaven and earth, something not always preached to the unbeliever, but which we should always keep in mind.

Overall there are many reasons to hold the book of Ecclesiastes in high regard. One is that it reminds us of the need for our faith to be robust enough to stand up to the realities of this world and to face life's uncertainties and perplexities. Without this resilience, our faith can remain shallow, as well as being open to criticism by those who find it difficult, or even impossible, to accept any kind of belief in God for themselves.

In the final analysis we should admire Qoheleth for many things, not least his honesty and realism. He asks awkward questions because he knows that life asks these questions of all of us. He is prepared to grapple with the troublesome problems of life, ageing and death, and he does so with integrity and depth, but, as we have seen, he can only work with what he can observe within a this-worldly horizon. As a result he accepts that the search for total knowledge is futile and that a humble acknowledgment of mystery is necessary. Such humility should be our watchword too.

God's actions in this world can never be reduced to neat rules or simple formulae. His will is often mysterious and even unsettling.

Qoheleth is a special kind of teacher, one who would rather confront inconvenient facts than simply repeat pious-sounding clichés. In that sense, he is a rebel. He works within the wisdom tradition yet he also calls it into question by refusing to stand with the orthodox whose well-rehearsed platitudes may mean well but which could ultimately be, in Qoheleth's own memorable phrase, 'Meaningless! Meaningless! Utterly meaningless!'

Ecclesiastes is a fascinating work of Hebrew wisdom. Both Judaism and Christianity accord this book a place in their sacred writings. Both would be poorer without it. But although Ecclesiastes rightly secured its status among the esteemed wisdom writings, it should not be read in isolation from the rest of the Old Testament wisdom books, or indeed now of the entire biblical canon.

Next we will consider how the three wisdom books we have studied so far – Proverbs, Job and Ecclesiastes – might relate to each other.

Chapter Twenty-Four

The Relationship Between Proverbs, Job and Ecclesiastes

In this chapter we will highlight the relationship between the three wisdom books of the Old Testament we have been studying: Proverbs, Job and Ecclesiastes. We have already seen that there are significant differences between these three books, but how do they relate to each other within the overall wisdom tradition?

When comparing books and seeking associations between them, one aspect is that of chronology. If we know which was written first then we can look for signs as to how this might have affected later books. However, in our separate studies of the three wisdom books we have seen how difficult it is to conclude when each of them was written or finally compiled. Indeed, in general, the precise dating of any single piece of wisdom material, whether an individual proverb or a larger work, is, by its very nature, largely elusive. Wisdom is not that time-specific. While such chronological uncertainties may not affect our appreciation of the message of any particular piece of wisdom, it can hinder attempts to determine how such pieces relate to each other.

Another important feature for consideration when comparing books is that of references to one book within another. For instance, are there any quotations from one to another, or any common references to a third book? In the case of Proverbs, Job and Ecclesiastes, none of them quote directly from any other, which may also seem to inhibit a search for precedence or interdependence.

However, all is not lost in this respect. Proverbs of various kinds were in circulation from the time of Solomon onwards, if not earlier. This particular format for passing on wisdom not only flourished during the period of the early monarchy but also continued throughout the rest of the Old Testament era. So we can be sure that individual proverbs existed before Job and Ecclesiastes were written (or finally compiled), even if the biblical book of Proverbs was yet to be produced. Indeed, we saw in previous chapters that Ecclesiastes contains several statements of a proverbial nature and that part of Qoheleth's role as a Teacher was to search out and set in order many such proverbs (Eccles. 12:9-10). There are also parts of Job that reflect the style and content of proverbs (see Job 5:2, 18:5ff).

This gives us a scenario in which Proverbs represents a constant and regular form of wisdom which occurs over a long period, whereas Job and Ecclesiastes are one-offs, entering into the wisdom tradition at some point in history, even if that exact point remains unknown. In addition, if the book of Proverbs represents the conventional norm, then the other two books are more individual and atypical, even to the point of reacting against this norm. But in what way are they reactionary?

Wisdom literature divides into two basic kinds, the simple orthodoxy found in the book of Proverbs, and the more questioning approach of Job and Ecclesiastes. The former displays full confidence in the just outworking of God's assigned earthly rewards and punishments; the latter undertakes a severe cross-examination of this view of reality.

Those who compiled proverbs undertook to discover the means of making life-enhancing choices. If we make wise decisions, all will go well; if we make foolish decisions, all will go badly. The wisdom in Proverbs affirms a divinely directed moral order at work in human life in which the wise and good are rewarded, while the foolish and wicked incur appropriate punishment. Job and Ecclesiastes are then seen as being 'wisdom in revolt', a sharp protest against such naïve optimism. There are two opinions as to how this works out.

One is that Job reacts against the hard and fast rules that Proverbs advocates, and then Ecclesiastes comes along and reacts even further against both Proverbs and Job. It protests yet more strongly with even fiercer questions, reducing life to a pointless display of activity in a meaningless world which leads only to death.

However, there is another view which states that Ecclesiastes and Job are both reacting against Proverbs separately and in different ways. This removes any suggestion that one of them (Ecclesiastes) is also in dispute with the other (Job). This is the more common way of assessing the overall relationship between the three books as we now have them in our scriptures. As we read them today, here is a simultaneous two-pronged attack upon Proverbs rather than a successive assault which developed over time.

This second position does seem to be the most likely, but we must not assume this is a full onslaught aimed at completely destroying proverbial wisdom. This form of wisdom may need to be questioned and critiqued, but not undermined to the point of demolition. Both Job and Ecclesiastes need the firm basis provided by Proverbs upon which to make their own points. It is not in their own interest to dismantle it completely. Qoheleth makes some of his sharpest observations in reaction to the clear-cut axioms of Proverbs. His scepticism requires Proverbs to remain true to a large extent otherwise his own case falls apart and becomes meaningless too.

Job also upholds the fundamental premises of proverbial wisdom but subjects it to radical criticism of a particular kind. The book makes us realise there is more to understand about the depths of the divine-human relationship which traditional wisdom cannot reach. There is an ultimate mystery which will always remain beyond its parameters. We must recognise this and accept it, however disconcerting it may be. The riddles of human existence and suffering cannot be resolved by conventional wisdom, only through divine self-revelation and a continual trust that God is good. This is a vital part of being wise.

If Job is the search for God's presence, the pursuit of God within times of the greatest darkness and despair, then Ecclesiastes is the search for ultimate meaning within life as a whole. But, unlike in Job, in Ecclesiastes there is no dialogue between Qoheleth and God. Perhaps for this reason Qoheleth never finds any real satisfaction or resolution to his dilemmas. His conclusion is therefore to revert to the proverbial wisdom of fear God and keep his commandments (Eccles. 12:13), while enduring the continual distress and wretchedness of a life without meaning. Job, on the other hand, suffered more intensely for a while, and was greatly impacted by a loss of health, wealth and family, but his encounter with God brought him some kind of finality. He gained a deeper wisdom. So perhaps it is fair to conclude that, compared to Qoheleth, Job had a better experience. Even though his circumstances were more devastating, ultimately his despair was more fruitful and life-enhancing.

To draw these thoughts together a bit more, we have seen that wisdom is primarily about gaining a correct understanding of reality. This presupposes a coherent and divinely ordained order within creation that can be perceived. This is fundamental to all kinds of wisdom. From this starting point, various strands of wisdom emerge. Proverbs asserts that given the right start in life through a healthy fear of the Lord, a person can be instructed to live a good life in the right way. Job then says that this pursuit of understanding, while not wrong in itself, may, and indeed will, encounter deep mysteries that do not fit into any general scheme and which will throw us back onto trusting the unseen goodness of God. Ecclesiastes adds another perspective by reflecting on how human nature and wickedness has confused this divinely ordained order to such an extent that a rigid interpretation of wisdom on all life's experiences will lead us into greater despair, a despair that is different from that of Job but no less real and even more long lasting.

It seems there were always radical thinkers who were less willing to accept the glib assurances of the orthodox, and so two divergent tendencies within the wisdom tradition resulted: one conservative, the other more sceptical. This kind of debate was seen as healthy and so when the third part of the Jewish canon, the Writings, was added to the central core of Torah and the prophets, both types of wisdom literature were seen as necessary and so were included.

Having three such diverse books within the same section of their canon is a typical Hebraic approach. We might prefer to synthesise them into one larger book containing a comprehensive coverage of all the various facets of wisdom. But this would defeat the overall object. It is more beneficial to have separate books, each with a single-minded pursuit of their own respective viewpoint. Each book can then give itself wholly to one perspective and speak with maximum force, leaving any resulting imbalance to be corrected in due course by an equally forceful counterweight. This approach is easier to comprehend than one large volume full of many-sided arguments that get in each other's way, with every statement being qualified or countered the moment it is made, which would only create more confusion to these already complex issues. In addition, a single volume could come across as a compromise, a kind of merged average in which all the main arguments are diminished or even lost altogether. Far better is to listen to each book in turn, allowing each to ring true in its own way. Individually, each book is fascinating, but taken together their power grows exponentially once we realise how they relate to each other and we are not put off by their differences.

Some commentators say that Job and Ecclesiastes represent 'wisdom in crisis', but this is greatly overstating the case. They play just as constructive a role as Proverbs. Together the three books exist in creative tension, each helping interpret the other. Collectively, they provide a fuller wisdom but one which does not try to explain all of life. Indeed, they act as a warning to anyone attempting such a complete explanation, and rebuke the arrogance of those who claim to have succeeded in this.

Studying the relationship between these three wisdom books has shown us that, as a whole, the biblical wisdom literature incorporates a self-critical element and is prepared to examine its own arguments. Indeed, even Proverbs is not blind to the harsher problems of life and does occasionally question itself to some extent, though not as strongly as either Job or Ecclesiastes which will never allow the injustices and inequalities of life to be ignored or seen as trivial.

These aspects of the biblical wisdom tradition also provide valuable lessons for us as Christians. Our faith must also operate within the same tensions. For instance, we can know with absolute conviction our final goal with its resolution of all ills, yet at the same time have no certainty about what tomorrow will bring. We must constantly live in the awe and mystery of both knowing and not knowing. We may prefer things to be systematic and neat, but we cannot rewrite the Bible in that image. Instead we must accept that within its truth there remain strange paradoxes. We need a faith that can cope with messiness, unpredictability and irreconcilable complexities.

In this chapter we have been asking how three very different books relate to each other within the overall framework of biblical wisdom. Despite the bold juxtaposition of very different ideas, perhaps we should conclude that these three books are conversation partners. In the end, none of them wins through at the expense of the others, or has the final say. No single one provides the final truth. Instead we have more than one lens to provide a rich and rounded view of reality. Each is true but not the whole truth.

In the next chapter we will move on from these three main books and see what else there is to learn about wisdom in the rest of the Old Testament, especially the Psalms.

Chapter Twenty-Five

Wisdom in the Psalms

We have spent a lot of time on the three main wisdom books of the Old Testament – Proverbs, Job and Ecclesiastes – but it would be rather strange if the characteristics of wisdom were absent from the rest of the Hebrew scriptures. In this chapter we will briefly consider wisdom elsewhere in the Old Testament, especially in the Psalms.

The first mention in the Bible of someone being wise is Joseph. He may not have always acted wisely in his early days when dealing with his family, but later he sufficiently impressed Pharaoh with his interpretation of dreams and his economic plans to avoid famine that the Egyptian ruler declared, 'There is no one so discerning and wise as you' (Gen. 41:39). More importantly, it was recognised that 'God has made all this known to you' and that this was due to the spirit of God (Gen. 41:38-39, also 41:16). Here is a first indication that true wisdom comes from God, and that its nature is both spiritual (interpreting dreams) and practical (running the national economy).

Another similarity with the wisdom literature is found in the Law where the Israelites are constantly told to fear or revere the Lord so that it might go well with them (see for instance, Deut. 5:29, 6:2, 24). Then in Amos there are many occurrences of the numerical proverb, those with the x, x+1 format which are found in the sayings of Agur (Prov. 30), though perhaps the prophet is using this in a slightly different way (see Amos 1:3, 6, 9, 11, 13, 2:1, 4, 6, 3:3-6).

Again, very significantly there is the wisdom displayed by Daniel, similar to that of Joseph regarding interpreting dreams and the ability to govern well. Daniel himself testifies: 'Praise be to the name of God for ever and ever; wisdom and power are his . . . He gives wisdom to the wise and knowledge to the discerning . . . you have given me wisdom and power' (Dan. 2:20-23, also v27). Once more we are left in no doubt as to the source of Daniel's wisdom.

When we turn to the psalms there is a specific type known as wisdom psalms. This category is designated as such as the psalms within it have a certain kinship with the three wisdom books, not so much based upon form or style but content. They display some of the themes prominent in Proverbs, Job or Ecclesiastes.

While there is agreement that wisdom psalms exist, there is far less consensus on the precise number of them or which ones should definitely belong to a core list. While there are a significant number of psalms which display features commonly associated with wisdom it is not clear how many such features a psalm must possess before it can fully qualify as a wisdom psalm. In addition, some scholars say certain psalms display wisdom influence, but this is not enough for them to be counted within the full category. All this illustrates the difficulty in classifying psalms in general. They weren't written to fit neatly into our prescribed types.

As any list is open to debate, we are not going to attempt one here. We don't have time anyway to study all those that do get the vote from most scholars, so instead we will select a handful that make a contribution towards our exploration of biblical wisdom so far.

As we have seen, the wisdom literature divides into the orthodox and the more questioning, so we would expect the same of the wisdom psalms. Some of them are similar to proverbial wisdom in that they mention divine rewards and punishments, and aim to point us in the direction of behaviour that is approved and blessed by God by drawing a contrast between a righteous lifestyle and a wicked one.

Psalm 1 is a good example of this with its strong distinction between virtue which brings prosperity, and vice which leads to disaster. Its opening verse refers to a man (or woman) being blessed, not just happy but able to receive a special blessing from God that can only come from walking in his way. Then there is a mention in verse 2 of the law. Meditating constantly on this gift from God leads to success in life. The psalm generally follows the style of Proverbs by exhorting and admonishing, and it ends in verse 6 with a statement so similar to what we find in the book of Proverbs that it could have been lifted directly from it: 'For the LORD watches over the way of the righteous, but the way of the wicked leads to destruction.'

Psalm 111 ends with the motto text of Proverbs, that the fear of the Lord is the beginning of wisdom (Ps. 111:10), and seems to form a pair with Psalm 112, which also contrasts the righteous with the wicked based upon the wisdom that comes from fearing the Lord.

The wisdom books often connected wisdom with the Torah, as do several psalms, such as Psalm 1 mentioned above. The best example though is Psalm 119, which praises God for providing the means by which his people can live well. It celebrates this gift of wisdom by proclaiming a love for it and by exhorting the need to cultivate a devotion to the study of Torah. This psalm is primarily about courting wisdom and pursuing a sincere relationship with it.

Psalm 78 establishes itself as a wisdom poem from its opening call to 'hear my teaching; listen to the words of my mouth' (Ps. 78:1). Verse 2 follows with references to parables and hidden things, which are usual indicators of wisdom material. Overall, in verses 1 to 3 we have a wisdom teacher demanding our attention. He is about to instruct us, yet this instruction is very different from that in the wisdom books themselves. Instead we are treated to a recital of Israel's salvation history. Here is how wisdom is to be gained, by learning from the past. It seems Psalm 78 is a retelling of historical events in order to make them the subject of a lesson in wisdom. Paul was to say something similar in Romans 15:4, 'For everything that was written in the past was written to teach us.' Also in 1 Corinthians 10:1-11 Paul states that what happened in the past to Israel serves as warnings for us.

As we said earlier, some psalms follow the orthodoxy of proverbs but others are more questioning in their approach. They wrestle with issues of suffering and doubt, and so have more in common with Job and Ecclesiastes, though none are as vigorous as either of these.

Psalm 49 is another one that opens with a call to attention because words of wisdom are about to be spoken or even sung (v1-4). Here is a riddle, a deep and puzzling question that requires rigorous thought. The psalmist is about to tackle the commonly discussed problem of the prosperity of the wicked and the suffering of the righteous, but claims he will do so with fresh understanding and extra wisdom.

Like Qoheleth in Ecclesiastes, the psalmist observes that all come to the same end, rich and poor. So why fear rich and powerful enemies when they will eventually come to nothing? The righteous will one day be vindicated and prevail over the wicked. Then, in verse 15, comes a surprise. The psalmist declares that, while the wicked will continue to decay in their graves, God will ransom him from Sheol, the realm of the dead. He has glimpsed something that evaded Qoheleth, who we saw earlier was limited to this world and this life. Did the psalmist get this revelation by engaging in conversation with God in a way that Qoheleth didn't? We cannot tell, but clearly here is faith in God to redeem: 'He will surely take me to himself.' We may not be sure how he understood this redemption and afterlife but it gave him confidence to face the trials of this life and teach this to others.

The final psalm we will look at is Psalm 73, one of several by Asaph. We will consider this in some detail as it also has similarities with Job and Ecclesiastes and shows once again how the simple deed-outcome concept of Proverbs is challenged by the realities of life. Here is another honest psalm which admits that quite often evil men prosper and good men suffer adversity.

Asaph starts positively by affirming his faith in God. Here is his creed: God is good, and especially so to his own people. This is fundamental to him. In fact he starts very emphatically with 'Surely'. Surely this is so. This the first of three times he uses this word 'surely'. We will come across the other two in due course.

However, having started with this strong declaration, Asaph feels that it is being put to the test. He continues with a 'But'. In particular, 'But as for me . . .' He describes himself as slipping and sliding, losing his footing and about to fall. Why does he feel like this?

What he sees in the world around him doesn't match what he believes. Here is a real tension. He believes God is fair and just but life doesn't seem to reflect this. In fact, the very opposite seems to be true. The wicked get away with things, and even prosper. They have no problems, no struggles; they remain healthy and wealthy (v4-5).

Of course, they do have struggles and illness like anyone else. He is exaggerating as his view is distorted by the tension he is feeling. His eyes are winning out; his thinking is skewed. He isn't just having a few doubts though; he is on verge of giving up. In verse 13 there is his second 'Surely'. He feels his own righteousness is in vain. What are the benefits of being pure? He is the one suffering, not the wicked.

Even worse is that the wicked scoff at God because he doesn't seem to do anything to oppose them. So they are carefree. They continue to go their own way, and even attract others as they are doing so well (v6-11). In the end, this is all too much for Asaph. It is like a huge weight crushing him, and he is deeply troubled (v16).

So far Asaph's experience had been like that of Qoheleth. But things were about to change. One day he entered the sanctuary of God (v17), which some translations render as the secret, or secret place, of God. Of course Asaph would have entered God's sanctuary before, even on a regular basis, but this time as he went into God's presence, he heard God's thoughts on all this, and then he understood! Rather than thinking about things in terms of his own understanding, Asaph encountered a new wisdom, a heavenly wisdom.

As with Job, it was the presence of God which was transformational. Asaph had not physically suffered as Job had, but his mental anguish was almost as great. Why is this happening? Why is the world like this? Asaph had found no help in human wisdom, either religious or philosophical, but he did find answers once he listened to God.

Unlike Job, who was bombarded with question after question, Asaph most likely heard the gentle whispering voice of God's Spirit offering him comfort and understanding. What did he hear that made all the difference and brought some kind of resolution to his mind?

In verse 17 Asaph says, 'Then I understood their final destiny.' He suddenly saw further ahead. His view changed from short term to long term. Things will not always be like this. There is an ultimate justice. Trusting what our eyes see gives us a limited perspective; trusting God gives us his perspective, together with a realisation that his thoughts and his ways are higher than ours. We may not be able to understand them but we can know that they are there.

Then comes his third 'Surely' (v18). They are on slippery ground, not me! The poetic form of the psalm reverts back to verse 2 in its imagery.

He admits that when he was full of grief and bitterness he couldn't see things properly. He was senseless, ignorant, like a brute beast (v21-22). But now he has been enlightened.

From verse 23 onwards he again declares his faith but with even more certainty than in verse 1. He has come through to a firmer faith. His feet are back on solid ground. He has gained a deeper knowledge of God and his ways. The wicked will be cast down, suddenly destroyed and completely swept away (v18-19), but Asaph also knows that he will always be with God and is destined for glory (v23-24). He can declare that God is the strength of his heart and his portion forever (v26).

The final verse, verse 28, reflects the opening of the psalm, with 'But as for me' referencing back to verse 2, and his use of the word 'good' reminding us of how he started in verse 1. He can now also tell others of what he has learnt about how God operates. Previously, in his state of anguish and depression, he had not dared to speak out (v15).

This psalm shows us that entering the presence of God puts us in touch with the wisdom of God, and that this contrasts greatly with the best wisdom that man can produce.

In our next chapter we will look at wisdom in the Apocrypha, those books which didn't get into the canon of scripture.

Chapter Twenty-Six

Wisdom in the Apocrypha

We noted earlier that there were two wisdom books well known to the Jewish people which didn't get into their canon of scripture. These are the Wisdom of Solomon and the Wisdom of Jesus Ben Sirach, or just Sirach for short, also known as Ecclesiasticus, from Jerome's Latin version of the Bible. Although we are only considering biblical wisdom, it is worth spending a little time on these two books in order to have a brief idea of what is in them and also to think more about why they weren't included.

As these books are not in the Jewish canon, they are not included in the Protestant Bible but placed instead in a separate collection of books called the Apocrypha, which means 'hidden away' or 'secret', as though they were not allowed to be out in the open for all to see or read. However, they are part of both the Catholic and the Eastern Orthodox Bibles where they are categorised as Deuterocanonical, or second canon. However, this means they can still be read alongside the biblical wisdom books, which might lead readers to understand them also as being 'scripture'. Meanwhile, the Anglican tradition clarified its position in Article 6 of the 39 Articles of 1562 by stating that these books can be read for 'example of life and the instruction of manners' but not 'to establish any doctrine'.

We turn first to the Wisdom of Solomon, a title that reflects the standpoint of the book but which does not mean it was written by Solomon or associated with him directly in any way. As we have seen before (for instance, regarding Ecclesiastes), Solomon was so revered and associated with wisdom that his name was often attached to various books of wisdom. But whereas with Ecclesiastes we had to argue carefully that Solomon was not the author, here it is much clearer. For a start, the original text is not in Hebrew but in Greek. The author seems fully at home in that language, making use of Greek rhetoric and philosophical terms. Overall, the book displays many Hellenistic features and influences. It also contains quotations from the Septuagint, the Greek version of the Old Testament, which means it cannot have been written before 200 BC at the earliest. Scholars therefore tend to date it towards the end of the first century BC, though some say even later, after AD 30. All of this makes the book's association with Solomon a more artificial device than in Ecclesiastes. But just as Qoheleth in Ecclesiastes briefly wears the mantle of Solomon in order to explore the experiences only a king could enjoy, so this anonymous author allows himself to be Solomon's mouthpiece for a specific purpose. What would that be?

The book is commonly regarded as having its origins in Alexandria, the main centre of Hellenistic Judaism. The unknown author was most likely a Hellenistic Jew himself, living there as part of the dispersion. As such he was capable of writing for those immersed in Greek culture while also personally maintaining strong ties with the Jewish faith. Rather than being a compendium of instructions for pupils (such as in Proverbs or, as we shall see, in Sirach), this book is an extended treatise, an essay in apologetics designed for a wider audience of both Jews and Gentiles. It has two aims. One is to bolster the faith of the large Jewish community now living in the alien Greek culture. The other is to present the Jewish faith and wisdom to the Gentile world, especially to its rulers. Essentially the author is making a case for Hebrew wisdom in the face of Greek intellectualism.

The book divides into three parts: chapters 1 to 5, chapters 6 to 9 and finally chapters 10 to 19. The opening verse addresses the rulers of the earth, but the rest of part one seems more suited to a Jewish audience as it contains ideas and terms that are Hebraic and biblical and which would make less sense to Gentile readers.

In part two, the author picks up his call to the rulers of the earth, this time summoning them to listen and learn (6:1). Now he directly assumes the role of Solomon, the king who set his heart on wisdom and desired it above all else. Here he addresses his fellow monarchs throughout the world. Wisdom brought me great success. Don't you want the same? Everyone in power should seek the same wisdom from God that Solomon had. Reasons for this are then given, namely that all human sovereignty is delegated by God, governing is a sacred task, and all rulers are ultimately accountable to God. In addition there is the fact that such wisdom is readily available to all who desire it. The author also outlines the nature of wisdom and lists many of its attributes and qualities in an attempt to attract non-Jews towards the faith of Israel and the God of Israel.

If this was the case with the Queen of Sheba, then why not other foreign rulers?

The main feature of this central section is to show how Solomon became wise, not by a special birth (he was human like anyone else) or by personal attainment, but by a gift from God. The author, writing as Solomon, recounts how in his youth he became enamoured of wisdom for her excellence and special qualities. We are told of Solomon's love for wisdom and desire to have her as his bride. He pursued her as he would a beloved; she responded, and marriage ensued. This marriage between wisdom and Solomon is another example of personification, which we have seen before in other biblical books. Here this literary device is used to explain how Solomon became so wise. This central section culminates in chapter 9 with Solomon's prayer for wisdom that will enable him to rule and judge fairly. This draws freely upon the account of his dream and prayer at Gibeon found in 1 Kings 3:5-15.

The final and longest section contains ten chapters in which the author emphasises how wisdom guided God's chosen people from the very beginning, from Adam through to Moses, via Noah, Abraham, Lot, Jacob and Joseph. We are taken at great speed through these examples from Genesis in order to spend more time on the events of the Exodus. In some ways, these chapters form a midrash or interpretative commentary on the Exodus, highlighting the contrast between God's dealings with Israel and with the Egyptians. It was wisdom that led Israel safely out of Egypt and through the wilderness. At one point, wisdom is even identified as the cloud that accompanied them by day and the pillar of fire by night.

Overall, this is a fascinating book illustrating how by this time in their history, the wisdom of the Hebrews had been shifted into an alien context, and how the author tries to promote biblical wisdom within this new realm of Greek philosophical thought.

We turn now to the other apocryphal wisdom book, that of Jesus Ben Sirach, which is much longer, containing fifty-one chapters in total. According to his own words in 50:27, his full name was Jesus son of Eleazar son of Sirach, and he lived in Jerusalem. The original language of the book was Hebrew and he completed it around 180 BC, though it was probably composed in two or more stages over a period of time between 190 and 180 BC. It has become common to refer to the author as Ben Sira, and his book as Sirach, which we will do here in order to distinguish between them.

Elsewhere in the book we learn that Ben Sira was well travelled and that he was a scholar and teacher of the Law who gathered pupils around him, perhaps in his own school of instruction in Jerusalem. Of particular interest is that before the original first chapter, there is a prologue or preface, written several decades later in Greek by Ben Sira's grandson. He wrote this in Alexandria sometime after 132 BC. We know this as within the prologue he refers to the fact that he came to Egypt in the thirty-eighth year of Ptolemy VIII, also known as Euergetes II, which equates to 132 BC. But he didn't just provide a prologue. At the same time, he translated the whole book from the original Hebrew into Greek. This was to make it available to the Jewish community in Alexandria. It is this Greek translation which is the only complete text to have survived. Although large parts of the original Hebrew text have been recovered, this amounts to at most two thirds of the whole, so English translations today are made from the Greek version of Ben Sira's grandson.

In style and outlook, Sirach is very similar to the book of Proverbs. It makes several references to the fear of the Lord, and includes the familiar motto phrase that to 'fear the Lord is the beginning of wisdom' (1:14). As in Proverbs, Ben Sira addresses the reader as 'my son', providing him with moral instruction and exhortation to faith through the usual format of pithy traditional sentence-sayings. Again like Proverbs, the book explores the idea of wisdom both as a way of life for us to follow and as a divine reality at work in the created world and human life. In other words, the book not only offers isolated nuggets of wisdom but also shows how wisdom itself is part of God and his activity. For instance there is a poem on wisdom's role in creation which reminds us of Proverbs chapter 8.

In particular, Ben Sira reinforces the long tradition of a proverbial wisdom which is to be passed on from father to son and studied diligently. These sayings embody the truth of past generations. They have been tested and found reliable. Much effort went into their formulation and they are not to be discarded readily. However, Ben Sira was more than just a compiler of ancient wisdom material for the instruction of young people. He reformulated older sayings in his own words, added new ones, and developed others into miniature essays.

But there are also several significant differences between Sirach and the book of Proverbs. For instance, Sirach asserts that through the gift of Torah a special association was created between divine wisdom and Israel. Moreover, whereas the three main biblical wisdom books avoid any allusion to Israel's history as recorded elsewhere in scripture, Ben Sira draws upon this rich heritage to illustrate wisdom at work. Indeed, he uses it significantly in the final chapters. In general, Ben Sira intersperses the proverbs and precepts with worship, theology and devotional mediations. Overall, this suggests the book has been carefully constructed, more so than Proverbs, as illustrated by the following analysis.

The first section occupies nearly half the book, from the opening verse all the way through to 24:29. This large section begins and ends with two meditations on the nature and divine origin of wisdom (1:1-20, 24:1-29). Between these come groups of proverbs which are in turn regularly interrupted by other features. The first three of these are poems in which wisdom is pictorially personified (4:11-19, 6:18-31, 14:20–15:8). Later there is a meditation on the work of God in creation (16:24–18:14), and finally a prayer in 22:27–23:6.

The next section runs from 24:30 to 39:11. Here another long series of proverbs is interrupted twice, first by a meditation in 33:7-15, and then by a psalm of supplication in 36:1-17. The whole is brought to a conclusion with a long essay contrasting the privileged career of a scholar with other occupations (38:24–39:11).

The final main section is from 39:12 to 50:24. It starts with a call to praise the Creator and later features a hymn of praise (42:15–43:33) with some short wisdom essays in between. Then comes the most famous part of the book, the only bit which occasionally gets a public reading, usually from the King James Bible. It opens with: 'Let us now praise famous men and our fathers that begat us.' Many people have heard this without knowing where it comes from. Thus begins a lengthy recital of the names and deeds of men of faith from Enoch to Nehemiah, occupying six whole chapters (44 to 49). This is followed in chapter 50 by a tribute to the recent High Priest Simon ben Onias, which includes a description of the Temple service on the Day of Atonement.

The final chapter, chapter 51, is in two parts, starting in verses 1-12 with a psalm of thanksgiving and followed by an autobiographical section in which the author invites prospective pupils to come and dwell in his house of learning (v13-30). But this is not necessarily everything we might read. In some English versions, inserted between these two halves of the final chapter, there is yet another poem entreating us to give thanks to the Lord. This, it seems, occurs in the original Hebrew text but not in the Greek translation by Ben Sira's grandson, so it may not always be included in English versions of the book.

Overall, the book of Sirach reflects the more orthodox Jewish view of wisdom. In this way it is similar to the book of Proverbs, perhaps too similar.

In the end, the two books we have been considering in this chapter were excluded from the Jewish canon, whereas Proverbs, Job and Ecclesiastes were included. Would that have been our choice? If we had been asked to select just three of these five, would Job and Ecclesiastes have been on our list? Or would we have been tempted to leave out one, or both, of these more demanding books in favour of the 'easier' wisdom books of Solomon or Jesus Ben Sirach?

But as we saw earlier, Proverbs, Ecclesiastes and Job belong together to provide a balanced approach to the whole topic of wisdom. They interact with each other, and challenge each other, in a way that three similar books could never do. Three books of the same kind as Proverbs could only result in a blandness which the Bible would never allow.

Chapter Twenty-Seven

Learning from Solomon

We have already met Solomon several times in this book so far. Now we will ask just how wise he really was and what we can learn from him.

Mention the name of Solomon and certain things immediately come to mind: wealth, women, wisdom – three 'w's before it was usual to follow this by 'dot com'! A fourth could be added: writing. As we have seen not everything 'by Solomon' was actually by him in that sense, though some of it most definitely was.

Solomon gained a reputation of being the wisest man of his time, yet he also caused dissatisfaction among his people during his reign, and after his death there was rebellion and his kingdom split. So what should we conclude about this man and the wisdom he displayed?

Firstly, some facts. He reigned from 970 to 930 BC, the third King of Israel. He was the tenth son of his father, King David; his mother was Bathsheba. They named him Solomon, or Shlomo, meaning 'peace', though God sent word through Nathan the prophet that he should be named Jedidiah, meaning 'loved by the Lord' (2 Sam. 12:24-25).

His reign is recounted in the first eleven chapters of 1 Kings and the parallel passage of 2 Chronicles chapters 1 to 9. But we need to start further back, to a caution issued earlier by Samuel. When Israel first wanted a king, Samuel warned them that a powerful ruler could be selfish and abusive. Rather than him serving them, they would lose their sons and daughters to his service. He would take over their fields, olive groves and vineyards, and take the best of their herds and flocks for himself. Israel would cry out for relief, but to no avail (1 Sam. 8:11-18). Solomon's legacy was that he had indeed put a heavy yoke upon his people (1 Kgs 12:4), mainly through harsh conscripted labour of 183,000 men (1 Kgs 5:13-18). This was in order to build the Temple, something else he was to be remembered for.

As mentioned before, Solomon's wisdom was not a natural attribute or a personal attainment. It was a specific gift from God. As recorded in 1 Kings chapter 3, God appeared to Solomon in a dream at Gibeon and said, 'Ask for whatever you want me to give to you.' I wonder what we would have asked for! Solomon's response was one of humility. He recognised that ruling was a demanding task, so he asked for a discerning or listening heart to administer justice. He also requested the ability to distinguish between good and evil, literally to have penetrating insight to be able to tell the difference between the right path and the wrong path. Because he asked for wisdom, and not long life, wealth or the death of his enemies, God granted his request in abundance, and then gave him these other things as well!

One of the main roles of a king was to act as the nation's supreme judge, which involved bringing justice, fairness and peace into difficult situations. This was Solomon's motivation for asking for wisdom and it was soon put to the test.

The story of the two prostitutes and their two babies, one of whom had died overnight, is well known and a classic case of practical wisdom in operation (1 Kgs 3:16-28). As a narrative it is gripping in the way it is told and impressive in its end result. The argument between the two women is laid out before the king, who first of all sums up the dilemma using their own words. Then comes the command, 'Bring me a sword.' Imagine the tension mounting as one is fetched. What will he do with this? Rather than act, Solomon gives another order, a shocking instruction that would involve the death of the remaining child. But Solomon's wisdom is at work here, involving a simple piece of applied psychology and an insight into the maternal instinct, a compassion for their own child that few mothers would abandon. Of this, Solomon was completely confident, but it was still a risk. The result was more than just a satisfactory resolution to a tricky dilemma. Now all Israel 'held the king in awe, because they saw that he had wisdom from God to administer justice' (1 Kgs 3:28).

We read in the next chapter that God had given Solomon wisdom, very great insight and a breadth of understanding as measureless as the sand on the seashore, and that his wisdom was greater than all that of those of the East and of Egypt. As a result his fame spread to all the surrounding nations and many came from all around to listen to, and hopefully benefit from, his God-given wisdom (1 Kgs 4:29-34).

The most famous of these visits is that of the Queen of Sheba, as told in 1 Kings chapter 10. This unnamed Queen arrived from a distant land with many gifts plus several difficult questions to test out just how wise Solomon was. It seems he answered them all; nothing was too hard for him to explain to her (v3). As a result she was overwhelmed (v5). She confessed that the report about Solomon which had reached her country hadn't told her half of what she had just experienced, either regarding his wisdom or his wealth (v6-7). Her conclusion was to declare how happy people must be under his rule, especially those officials who serve at his court as they hear his wisdom daily (v8). She then gave him all the gifts she had brought and returned to her own country. End of story. Or is it?

There may well be something else hidden in this story. What did she really come for? The language is tantalisingly enigmatic at times. At the start, she 'talked with him about all that she had on her mind' (v2), and at the end Solomon gave her 'all she desired and asked for, *besides what he had given her out of his royal bounty*' (v13, italics mine). What could this be? Just some wise answers?

Some believe that part of her purpose for making such a long journey to meet Solomon was to become pregnant by him. Then once she knew she had conceived, she returned to her own country. Is this what was 'on her mind' and what they had talked about at the start of her visit? Is this what is meant by Solomon gave her 'all she desired'? If so, the biblical text prefers not to make this explicit, but there is some evidence to support this speculation from outside the Bible. According to a fourteenth-century epic of Ethiopia called the Kebra Nagast, the first emperor of Ethiopia, Menelik the First, was the son of Solomon and Queen Makeda of Ethiopia, who was the unnamed Queen of Sheba in the biblical account. Although the Kebra Nagast is a huge work full of seemingly legendary tales, might there be some truth in this part of it? It is not impossible that the Queen of Sheba wanted to start a dynasty of her own, and who better to help than Solomon? Perhaps she thought his wisdom would be inherited by her son? As for Solomon, would he have agreed to this? Quite likely, given his taste for foreign women! You can research this further for yourself sometime. Meanwhile, we return to the biblical text.

From the last part of 1 Kings chapter 4 we might think it must have been wonderful to have lived in Israel under Solomon's rule. Yet it all went wrong. Why? For part of the answer we need to go back to Deuteronomy chapter 17, where in verses 14 to 20 we find a description of what a king should be like and what he should do. Part of this is what he should *not* do. He must not acquire great numbers of horses for himself, or make people return to Egypt to get more horses. He must not take many wives who could lead him astray. He must not accumulate large amounts of silver and gold. Then there is what he *should* do. He is to write for himself a copy of the Law on a scroll. He is to read it every day and follow it. Moreover, he is not to consider himself better than his fellow Israelites, or turn from the Law in any way. How did Solomon do with regard to all this? Basically, badly in every respect.

In 1 Kings 10:14-25 we read that Solomon had a huge number of chariots and horses, mainly from Egypt. He accumulated large amounts of silver and gold; 666 talents of gold yearly and silver as plentiful as stones. He imported chariots from Egypt at a cost of 600 shekels of silver each, and horses at 150 shekels per head. He then exported them to the Hittites and Arameans, Israel's enemies. It seems he was an international arms dealer. Is this how he made so much money, by trading in weapons? Also, in Deuteronomy 7:1-2 God had told the Israelites not to make treaties with their enemies, including the Hittites, another part of God's law that Solomon disregarded.

In Deuteronomy 7:3, the Israelites were told not to intermarry with other nations, otherwise they would be turned away from following the Lord and end up serving other gods. However, Solomon took many foreign wives, probably justifying this by arguing that this enabled him to make alliances with other nations and secure peace. But this was at a great personal cost. They did indeed lead him astray, turning his heart away from the Lord his God (1 Kgs 11:1-4). As part of this, Solomon built high places just outside Jerusalem, pagan altars to the gods of his wives, for instance Chemosh the Moabite god and Molech the Ammonite deity (1 Kgs 11:7-8). Here they worshipped these false gods by burning their sons and daughters alive. Solomon was the first Israelite king to sacrifice his own children to Molech, those born to his foreign wives, all done in accordance with their own practices. This set a bad example to the whole nation for centuries to come.

Perhaps he did better when it came to the Temple which bears his name? Not really. God told David that he was not to build the Temple but his son would. However, it was David who was given instructions for this, who made preparations, and who provided resources from his personal treasure. Such was his devotion to the task. It was where his heart was. As a result the people followed in their giving, and there was great joy all round (see 1 Chr. chapter 22 and 29). David did all this so that Solomon could build the Temple from the moment he became king. But he didn't begin until the fourth year of his reign (1 Kgs 6:1, 37) and that was just the foundations. It took seven years in all. Meanwhile, Solomon had other priorities, including building his own palace. He took thirteen years over this (1 Kgs 7:1). Solomon's devotion to the Temple did not match that of his father David. Solomon's heart was elsewhere. However, that didn't stop him from taking all the credit. In his prayer of dedication in 2 Chronicles chapter 6, he repeatedly talks about the magnificent Temple *he* has built for God and for his Name. Five times he says 'I have built' (v2, 18, 33, 34, 38).

In 1 Kings chapter 9 God appears to Solomon a second time, just as he had before at Gibeon. He reminds him of the need for obedience, to walk in the ways of David, otherwise it will all have been in vain. The Temple would become a heap of rubble. When others see this, they will be appalled and God's people will become an object of ridicule among the nations. Did Solomon pay attention to this warning? All we know next is that after Solomon had built both the Temple and his Palace, he gave away part of the Promised Land to a foreign king! He gave Hiram, king of Tyre, twenty towns in Galilee in return for him having provided resources for these buildings. It seems Hiram wasn't thrilled with his reward for helping out, but it is unlikely that God was best pleased with this either (1 Kgs 9:10-13).

In summary, Solomon accumulated for himself gold, silver and horses; he made treaties with forbidden nations and married many of their women; he built pagan altars and endorsed child sacrifice; he sold weapons to Israel's enemies and gave away some of their own cities. He exalted himself above his brethren, and disregarded the very Law which he was to have copied, and read, and followed. Presumably he thought that with all his wisdom he knew better, that he was above these laws. They might apply to others but not to him. In doing all this he was also ignoring the wise advice of his father David who, in 1 Kings 2:2-4, warned his young son to 'observe what the LORD your God requires' in order for his kingdom to flourish.

So what can we conclude from all this? Overall, Solomon is a bit of a puzzle, a contradiction. Here is a complex character with two sides (at least), which the Bible doesn't attempt to reconcile. It leaves us to make our own decisions on him and learn lessons from his life. At first in the biblical account we are told his good points, but by the end negative assessments are made, preparing us for what is to come, namely the division and final destruction of his kingdom.

The tragedy of his story is summed up in two verses, one at the start (1 Kgs 3:3) where we read of 'his love for the LORD', though this was tainted by him also offering sacrifices and burning incense on the high places, and one at the end (1 Kgs 11:1) where we learn he 'loved many foreign women'. He had left his first love. Although he never stopped following Yahweh, there had been a gradual drift away until his heart was not fully devoted to the Lord his God, and he did not follow the Lord completely (1 Kgs 11:4, 6). Notice that in all these verses, including 1 Kings

3:3, David is also mentioned as though he provided the measure that Solomon was meant to live up to.

We can learn much from the life of Solomon. For instance, here is a warning that even great wise men can go astray. Those who acquire wisdom may not always use it wisely! In addition, just as Solomon may have thought his God-given wisdom allowed him to go against Torah, so our human wisdom may tell us we can ignore what God has said in his Word. Solomon may also have lost the sense of living in the fear of the Lord which would have kept him wise.

Wisdom is a great gift but it needs other things to sustain it. It also needs other people. Part of Solomon's problem was that he was the only such wise person around. It's not good for wisdom to be concentrated in just one person at the top. Clearly Solomon had lots of wisdom for others, but less for himself; he needed someone to be wise for him. Wisdom works better if it is spread around more. This is why in the New Testament it is widely available to all within the body of Christ. It is given to anyone who believes and asks for it. We all need to receive the gift of wisdom for the benefit of each other.

In the end, great as it was, Solomon's wisdom was not sufficient. Thankfully, as Jesus said, the Queen of Sheba may have come from the ends of the earth to listen to Solomon, but now 'something greater than Solomon is here' (Matt. 12:42). How far will we go to listen to the one who is indeed greater than Solomon – Christ himself, the wisdom of God?

Chapter Twenty-Eight

Christ, The Wisdom of God

In our previous chapter we considered Solomon, famed for being wise but who didn't always display that wisdom. But although we can learn much from studying his life, and probably those of many others in the scriptures, ultimately we must turn to the supreme example of Christ himself. As Paul declares in 1 Corinthians 1:24, Christ is 'the power of God and the wisdom of God'. An impressive accolade, indeed. But what do we make of this?

To speak of Christ as the wisdom of God is a complex matter. Many are attracted to Jesus simply as a wisdom teacher of high quality. They regard his words as purveying supreme examples of wise thinking. But that is as far as they go. They find wisdom in what he said, but do not believe in him as a divine person or trust him for their salvation. They might agree with Jesus' own words that when it came to wisdom, 'something greater than Solomon' was now here (Matt. 12:42, Luke 11:31) but they would not go along with Paul by calling Jesus 'the wisdom of God'.

Clearly Jesus' teaching displayed many aspects of the style of biblical wisdom. This is seen in his parables and also in his so-called Sermon on the Mount, especially in its final part with its many paired choices: two roads and gates, two trees and fruits, two kinds of hearers and house builders (Matt. 7:13-27). This pattern of injunction resembles parts of the book of Proverbs; for example, the two paths in Proverbs 4:11-19, and the two female companions and their houses in chapter 9.

Part of Jesus' mission was to challenge the folly of a humanity that had turned its back on the true wisdom of God. This included the folly he found among the religious leaders who should have known better. Jesus did not hesitate to expose this, even at one point attacking the Pharisees as 'You foolish people!' (Luke 11:40).

Moreover, as with any teacher of wisdom, Jesus urged his followers to act on what they knew to be right. Indeed, his whole call to discipleship encapsulated wisdom's call to choose the right course of action rather than that of folly, worldliness or immorality.

Given all this, it is not surprising to find in Luke 2:52 that from an early age 'Jesus grew in wisdom' as part of his human development. But his wisdom was not just the product of human learning, a sound upbringing or the later study of scripture. It came directly from the Father and also through the Holy Spirit. In a prophetic passage in Isaiah we read that 'the Spirit of the LORD will rest on him – the Spirit of wisdom and of understanding, the Spirit of counsel and of might, the Spirit of the knowledge and fear of the LORD' (Isa. 11:2). Here was an indispensable equipping to enable him to make full use of the literary tools of the wisdom of the past and to be a wisdom teacher in the tradition of the Old Testament. But he was much more than this. He embodied divine wisdom. He was the Wisdom of God not just by function, but by his very nature and person. He taught wisdom because of who he was.

Previously, in Proverbs, and especially in chapter 8, we met Lady Wisdom, a personification of wisdom which revealed new, and somewhat mysterious, elements of wisdom's origin and role at the start of creation. We made it clear then that this did not suggest Lady Wisdom was herself divine, part of the Godhead, or eternally pre-existent. Nor was Lady Wisdom being credited with a personal independent existence alongside God or being described as actively engaged in making the world. The writer was personifying a concept not describing a personality. He was using a poetic style to convey something of the way in which God's wisdom was involved in the creation of the world. However, it is clear that the language and imagery in Proverbs 8 has great depths and insights which, once we have knowledge of the incarnation, can be said to foreshadow a greater revelation to come in the New Testament.

It is always tempting to look back from the standpoint of the New Testament and seek to find Christ prefigured in the Old Testament as much as possible, but in this case there does seem to be a strong correlation between parts of Proverbs 8 and the opening lines of John's Gospel, as well as a significant theological development. In John, we have the eternal Logos, existing from the beginning and involved in creating all things. This Word (or Wisdom) of God was born into our world and lived among us in order to bring us, in his own person, a wisdom which would completely change lives forever.

Paul spells this out in more detail in some of his letters. As well as the statement in 1 Corinthians 1:24 that Christ is the wisdom of God, Paul adds in verse 30 that, for those who are in Christ Jesus, he has 'become for us wisdom from God'. Christ is always the wisdom of God but he becomes especially so for us once we are in him, meaning in a covenant relationship with him. Then this wisdom can flow into our lives and become ours. If we receive him, we receive his wisdom, his way of understanding the world and how to relate to God in it.

Something similar is found in Colossians 2:2-3, where Paul states that in Christ are 'hidden all the treasures of wisdom and knowledge'. But Paul wants us to realise that this is now available to those who have received Christ. This mystery of God is theirs to understand. In the scriptures the word 'mystery' is not a secret or riddle to be puzzled out, rather it means something hidden from us until revealed by God himself. This has now happened regarding the wisdom of God.

Also contained within this verse from Colossians is that in Christ are hidden all the treasures of *knowledge*, not just wisdom. Implied here is that the risen Jesus now has knowledge of all things, presumably in a way he did not when on earth in bodily form. It is interesting to speculate whether Jesus could have informed his disciples that the earth was not flat or that it orbited the sun and not vice versa. Could he have given lectures on quantum mechanics as part of his post-resurrection encounters with his followers? We would probably insist that this sort of knowledge was laid aside as part of his humanity as he limited himself to the constraints of the time. But what about now? We tend not to think of the risen Christ in intellectual terms, but perhaps among the other qualities of his glorification we should also regard him as the most intelligent person we can relate to. As such, his knowledge now extends to every domain of human life, every area in which modern knowledge is required. In short, Jesus is smart. And as our ever-living teacher, he can provide us with knowledge not just wisdom.

Meanwhile, we return to 1 Corinthians for it is in the first two chapters of this letter that we find the most concentrated exposition of wisdom in the New Testament. It is worth quoting some of this in full.

In 1 Corinthians 1:18-25 we read:

> 'For the message of the cross is foolishness to those who are perishing, but to us who are being saved it is the power of God. For it is written: "I will destroy the wisdom of the wise; the intelligence of the intelligent I will frustrate." [Isa. 29:14] . . . Has not God made foolish the wisdom of the world? For since in the wisdom of God the world through its wisdom did not know him, God was pleased through the foolishness of what was preached to save those who believe. Jews demand signs and Greeks look for wisdom, but we preach Christ crucified . . . Christ the power of God and the wisdom of God. For the foolishness of God is wiser than human wisdom, and the weakness of God is stronger than human strength.'

He continues in the second chapter of this letter:

> 'When I came to you, I did not come with eloquence or human wisdom . . . We do, however, speak a message of wisdom among the mature, but not

the wisdom of this age or of the rulers of this age, who are coming to nothing. No, we declare God's wisdom, a mystery that has been hidden and that God destined for our glory before time began.'
(1 Cor. 2:1, 6-7)

In these powerful and highly instructive passages, Paul describes two kinds of wisdom – human and divine – and maintains that they clash with each other. The wisdom of God is totally contrary to the wisdom of the world, specifically that of the Greek-thinking world, whether sophisticated speculations or fixed doctrines such as Gnosticism.

Paul states that the Greeks (Gentiles) seek wisdom, as indeed all men do, but they do not look in the right place. No-one can find true wisdom if they look to their own understanding and clever ideas rather than to God. Without the wisdom of God we can only struggle on with man-made wisdom, which ultimately leaves us floundering and open to deception and failure.

Paul also relates wisdom to the gospel and how it is to be preached. The gospel message is Christ crucified. This is contrary to both Jewish expectation and Greek wisdom. In the world's view the cross was an act of foolishness but in reality it was wiser than anything man could think of. As people find salvation through the crucified Christ, human wisdom appears foolish in comparison. Moreover, it is only through the wisdom of God that we can understand the cross. It makes no sense in human terms. In this way the wisdom of God has demoted worldly wisdom and turned it into foolishness. So Paul adds a warning that if we preach the gospel using human wisdom then the message of salvation loses its power. The gospel is not a new philosophical system to rival those of the Greeks. It is much more than any of these as it involves the wisdom of God.

In the Old Testament, wisdom was closely identified with creation and the order God had placed there. How to restore that order in a fallen world was the role of wisdom. But now, since Christ came to earth, was put to death and rose again in a new body, wisdom has gained a new redemptive element. It now moves us towards an even greater restoration, an even greater climax, the renewal of all things.

New Testament wisdom does not refute or dismiss the wisdom found in the Old Testament. It takes the same starting point, namely that man and the rest of creation are in disarray and in need of being restored. But it now has a different end point, a new creation altogether. We could say that it fulfils all previous wisdom and takes it further, with Christ himself providing the continuity between creation and re-creation.

Overall, the wisdom of God has put together an amazing plan for our salvation. Human wisdom may provide us with some limited meaning in terms of life now, but it can never match this. It may still have some good thoughts to offer our intellect but it remains at odds with the truth of how God established his creation, and how he intends to redeem it. Biblical wisdom is now about more than simply understanding the present confused disorder and living better within it. It is about a future restored order, and how to live in readiness for that. We can now view life beyond the here and now in a way that Qoheleth in Ecclesiastes could never have imagined.

Perhaps we should end with a verse from Paul's letter to the Romans, taking it slightly out of context, but it still applies.

> 'Oh, the depth of the riches of the wisdom and knowledge of God! How unsearchable his judgments and his paths beyond tracing out!' (Rom. 11:33)

Chapter Twenty-Nine

James and the Gift of Wisdom

In this chapter we turn to the letter of James and in particular that remarkable statement, 'If any of you lacks wisdom, you should ask God, who gives generously to all without finding fault, and it will be given to you' (Jas 1:5).

In many ways the letter of James is a strange one. It does not contain any of the great redemptive themes which we find in other letters. It does not explain the gospel or the saving work of Jesus. In fact, despite being Jesus' half-brother, James only mentions him by name twice, one of those being in the opening greeting; and there is no reference to the Holy Spirit. Yet if there is one book in the New Testament that could be categorised as wisdom literature, this is it.

Overall, James is deeply grounded in the wisdom literature of the Old Testament, especially that of the book of Proverbs with which his letter has many parallels, though only one direct quote (Prov. 3:34 in Jas 4:6). Like Proverbs, his letter lacks a clear structure or lengthy thematic development. It does have some short thematic sections, again similar to parts of Proverbs, but it is not a particularly orderly letter. It is more a compendium of wisdom, designed to continually exhort us to acquire true wisdom. In addition, his characteristic phrase 'Now listen' (4:13, 5:1) reflects the paternal concern in Proverbs that a son should listen to his father's instruction.

James was clearly influenced by previous wisdom material and yet his letter is also unmistakeably that of a follower of Jesus. Whatever he knew from the biblical wisdom tradition was filtered through the teaching of Jesus. For instance, he regularly echoes Jesus' Sermon on the Mount, itself reminiscent of Old Testament wisdom. Also, like Jesus, James urges us to put wisdom into practice, doing and not just hearing. He also calls on us to tame the tongue. Controlling what we say is again a theme common to Proverbs and the teaching of Jesus.

At one point James references Job in order to show the blessings of perseverance (5:11). But whereas Job's friends told him to repent, James tells us that when we face trials and testing, we should rejoice. Here is a different perspective. He had heard of Job's suffering, but he also knew of the sufferings of Christ who for the joy that was set before him endured the cross (see Heb. 12:2).

Two passages regarding wisdom stand out in the letter of James, namely 1:5-8 and 3:13-18. In the rest of this chapter and the next, we will look further into these. We start here with that amazing invitation quoted above, that 'If any of you lacks wisdom, you should ask God, who gives generously to all without finding fault, and it will be given to you' (Jas 1:5).

The Bible contains many wonderful offers, surely none greater than that found in Romans 6:23, where we read that the gift of God is eternal life in Christ Jesus our Lord. Some versions want to stress just how gracious God is by referring to it as a 'free gift' (see, for instance, the Revised Standard Version and the English Standard Version). Here in James we find that God's generosity extends to an amazing free offer of wisdom to all. Does this sound too good to be true?

For a start this is for everyone. If *anyone* lacks wisdom – that includes you, and me! And you don't need to pass any particular test or undergo any checks. There's no fault-finding involved. If you lack wisdom (and who doesn't at times!) then just ask, and free delivery is guaranteed. That's better than any supermarket offer. It's 'buy one, get one free' without even having to buy one. Who would want to turn that down?

But suspicions can set in. Is this genuine? Surely there must be a catch somewhere. We often argue that if something sounds too good to be true, it usually is! We tell ourselves, 'There's no such thing as a free lunch' or, if you come from the more northern parts of the United Kingdom, 'You don't get owt for nowt in this life.'

We should notice, however, that immediately after this wonderful offer of wisdom in the letter of James there is a sort of 'terms and conditions' clause attached, some small print to read over carefully. In the next verses, James goes on to issue a warning: 'But when you ask, you must believe and not doubt, because the one who doubts is like a wave of the sea, blown and tossed by the wind. That person should not expect to receive anything from the Lord. Such a person is double-minded and unstable in all they do' (Jas 1:6-8).

So something *is* required of us as part of our asking, namely a firm belief in the goodness of God to grant our request. But if you are a Christian then asking in faith is what you would normally do anyway. This is how a follower of Jesus should live, constantly believing that our heavenly Father provides us with every good and perfect gift (see Jas 1:17). We also have the words of Jesus himself to encourage us: 'Ask and it will be given to you; seek and you will find; knock and the door will be opened to you. For everyone who asks receives...' (Matt. 7:7-8).

It is no great surprise that James emphasises the faith aspect of asking for wisdom, as he insists in his letter that faith must show itself in action. Faith is not a passive state of mind, or something confined to a creed. Rather our faith is shown by how we live and act, and, in this case, by how we ask for what we need from our loving heavenly Father.

So, is this an offer you can't refuse? Will you take advantage of God's generosity? Sometimes there are certain obstacles within ourselves which need to be overcome before we reach out with glad and willing hands, or perhaps in this case with glad and willing minds, for it may well be our mindset that needs changing.

For instance, we might tell ourselves '*I* don't deserve this' or 'this can't include *me*'. We put ourselves down, based upon a low sense of self-worth or of God's love and provision for us. Alternatively, others may have too high a view of themselves. 'I can manage without anything from God. I've got enough wisdom of my own, thank you very much.' For still others, the main response to God's gift of wisdom might be indifference. 'Do I really need this? What use will it be anyway?'

Overall, there are many reasons why gracious gifts are turned down or passed over, even when they come from God. But in all cases, our hesitation in accepting or reluctance to receive in no way implies an unwillingness on God's part to be lavish in dispensing his gifts. If we lack wisdom, the problem is ours.

One major issue in this area of receiving from God lies in how we regard the Christian faith generally. In short, is Christianity a religion or a relationship? The essential difference between the special relationship with God that Christianity offers and religion in general can be described symbolically using two shapes. One is ∪ (a bit like a capital u), the other is its upside-down version, ∩, an arch-like curve.

In mathematical terms these are the symbols used in set notation to denote union and intersection respectively, often known as 'cup' and 'cap'. The ∩ shape depicts religion, where God is at the apex and humans are at the feet; God in heaven and us on earth, if you like. The idea represented here is that we must first offer something up to God before he will send anything down to us. We are required to please God, or even appease his anger, sending him a gift along the upslope in order that blessing might come down the other side to us. In the worst cases in certain pagan religions this might involve the sacrifice of a child. Overall, this deal-making approach means that if God accepts what we offer up to him, then we might get what we want in return, such as rain, crops, prosperity or success of some kind. This is the essence of a religious attitude.

Christianity, and indeed Judaism as it was intended, is the total opposite, and hence U-shaped. God is still at the top, but now at the two end points of the curve, and we are at the bottom, at the nose of the curve. God gives us something freely first. A gift comes down to us and once we receive what he has given us, we offer something (indeed our whole selves) back up to him in gratitude and service. This illustrates all aspects of Christianity, including salvation, eternal life and the gift of Christ himself, as well as the gift of the Holy Spirit. God always acts on our behalf first, then we respond back to him. This is grace in operation, a total contrast to contemporary life which is merit-based, performance-related and achievement-orientated, attitudes which shape just about everything we do. But if we apply this outlook to Christianity then we restrict ourselves in receiving anything from God, including wisdom.

A powerful motivation in asking for anything is developing a strong desire for it, even to the point of it becoming a serious ambition in life. When it comes to being wise, can we justify calling this an ambition? I think we can, and we should.

When I was younger I had an unusual ambition. I wanted to become a wise old man. That may seem a very strange ambition to have at such an early stage in life, but to me at the time it seemed rather a good one. For a start, I was already male, so there was nothing to do there. In addition, I was bound to get old just by staying alive; keep breathing and you get older with every breath you take. So I was already heading towards being an old man, rather slowly I hoped, but given that it was inevitable the only question was what kind of old man I would become. A sad old man? A grumpy old man? Being a wise old man seemed preferable. Moreover, I already knew enough of the Bible to recognise that this was also what God wanted for me and that wisdom was freely available if I would simply ask for it. So it became a lifelong ambition.

Of course, I also had other ambitions at that early age. I was going to open the batting for England, and between Test Matches I would travel the world as an international concert pianist. There was just one problem with these otherwise laudable ambitions – talent! Or rather, a lack of it! Apparently, a top score of 10 in a school match wasn't likely to qualify for England selection, and Grade 8 piano was not sufficient for top billing at the major concert halls of the world. So I had to abandon these worthy ambitions and be content instead with pursuing them as enjoyable and fulfilling hobbies.

But gaining wisdom seemed to be different. You didn't need a specific talent to become wise. It was being freely offered, and here was an offer I didn't want to refuse.

So what do you really desire in life? What is your ambition, however old or young you are? And will wisdom be part of this?

Chapter Thirty

Two Kinds of Wisdom

In this chapter we continue in the letter of James and focus on the passage which states that there are two kinds of wisdom, categorised as 'heavenly' and 'earthly', according to their origins. As such, they are fundamental opposites in their outlook on life, and completely at odds with each other.

We will start by quoting from the passage at length:

> 'Who is wise and understanding among you? Let them show it by their good life, by deeds done in the humility that comes from wisdom. But if you harbour bitter envy and selfish ambition in your hearts, do not boast about it or deny the truth. Such "wisdom" does not come down from heaven but is earthly, unspiritual, demonic... But the wisdom that comes from heaven is first of all pure; then peace-loving, considerate, submissive, full of mercy and good fruit, impartial and sincere.' (Jas 3:13-15, 17)

Here is a clear indication that the source of wisdom is important, and a warning that not all wisdom is from God. There is another kind of wisdom and this is described in very damaging and dangerous terms as unspiritual and demonic. In the version quoted above (NIV), the word for this earthly wisdom is put in quotation marks, as though the translators want to suggest that James is being ironic. He uses the same Greek word (*sophia*) but he is not prepared to give it the same status as heavenly wisdom. This 'so-called wisdom' is not really wisdom at all. Humans may think of it as such, but God does not.

This would also explain why James calls it unspiritual. It is not in any way from the Spirit of God. In fact, the word 'unspiritual' can also be translated 'sensual', meaning that this wisdom comes from our inner senses or desires, and develops within our own thinking independently of God. As such it is attractive to us and therefore prevalent within humanity. It suits us well. But this makes it dangerous, which is why James also describes it as demonic, partly to explain its origins and also to highlight that it can be used by God's enemies to keep us from God or to take us further away from him.

To understand this more we need to go back to the beginning, to Eden and the initial disobedience by Eve and then Adam. Whatever you make of the story as a whole, whether as a word-for-word factual account or a more poetic literary device to communicate truth, the principle involved here is clear. Eve saw that the forbidden fruit on the tree in the middle of the garden was not only 'good for food and pleasing to the eye' but also *'desirable for gaining wisdom'* (Gen. 3:6, italics mine).

The Hebrew for this last phrase is *nechmad lehaskiyl*, and is quite instructive. The word used here for wisdom is *haskiyl*, not the more common word *hakam*, though it has essentially the same meaning. The full term, *lehaskiyl*, gives us the phrase 'to make one wise'. Someone has coined the word 'enwisen' to describe this process, similar to words like enlighten or envision. This may accurately render the grammatical nature of the word but 'make you wise' or 'gain wisdom' will do just as well!

The first word in the phrase is particularly revealing. The Hebrew root of *nechmad* reflects a powerful driving force, a great urge to seize something you do not already possess, and is behind the word 'covet' as in the Ten Commandments (Exod. 20:17, Deut. 5:21).

As we have seen, there is nothing wrong with desiring wisdom but this is within the context of asking for it from God. In Eve's case, her desires had been stirred in the wrong direction by listening to the tempter, who probably made sure the tree was in her sightline when he began his conversation with her. Of course, Eve already knew the tree was there. She would have seen it before. It did rather stand out in the middle of the garden, and no doubt God had pointed it out when instructing them not to eat from it. But after the serpent had talked to her, Eve saw the tree differently and began to rethink. Here was a quick way to gain wisdom. Just take and eat. An easy option, but not the right one. This was grasping not asking. Taking for yourself is not the same as receiving what is offered.

Wisdom itself is not a forbidden fruit, but how you get it, and where from, matters. You cannot fast-track true wisdom in a way that is out of step with the Lord. In the end, for Adam and Eve, their action did not lead to greater wisdom but considerable confusion. It resulted in a loss of ability to see things as they really are and God as he really is.

The first humans thought they could achieve wisdom by exercising their independence, and we can be tempted to think the same when we look for wisdom elsewhere than from God. We should bear in mind what the Lord said in one of David's psalms: 'I will instruct you and teach you in the way you should go; I will counsel you with my loving eye on you' (Ps. 32:8).

Asking God for wisdom is part of having a continual relationship with him. His wisdom is not dispensed as a one-off gift, received in totality in a single delivery after which you can ignore God. All done! I've now got the gift and am completely wise in everything! Rather, true wisdom comes from walking with God over the course of a lifetime where you keep asking for more wisdom whenever you need it.

For Adam and Eve, seeking wisdom independently of God ultimately meant losing that special relationship with him which would have brought them true heavenly wisdom. In addition, their approach was close to being idolatrous in that they were desiring wisdom for itself rather than desiring God first and then receiving wisdom from him as a fatherly gift. We too must beware of making an idol out of wisdom as though all we really want is to hear people acclaim us as wise. Our motivation should be to seek wisdom for the service of God and others, not for self-promotion or personal honour and applause.

Basically, earthly wisdom omits God and his truth in favour of human ideas. Man is in control and can make his own decisions without reference to anything God has said or revealed about himself. The wisdom of this world looks at life as if God is not real or, perhaps worse, depicts him as a distorted caricature of what he is really like.

By contrast, heavenly wisdom is God telling us the real meaning of all that we see and do, in particular how life works when he is allowed to be in charge. By its nature, biblical wisdom is all-embracing and connective. On the other hand, earthly wisdom is fragmented, coming from many different human sources. Overall, it lacks the big picture. At best it can offer only a little help here and there. Most importantly, it cannot make us 'wise for salvation' (2 Tim. 3:15).

As we saw in a previous chapter when considering the writings of Paul, God has declared war on human wisdom and will ultimately destroy it. His wisdom may seem like folly to the wise people of this world. In their eyes the gospel is weak and foolish. But in reality it is the greater wisdom and will ultimately triumph.

Nevertheless, for now human wisdom remains a potent force. It dominates our world. We find it all around us, promoted by the education system, the entertainment industry and the media in all its forms. It heavily influences us, and we still find it tempting and have to resist it. Nor can we remain neutral in these matters.

However, the solution is simple. We need to exchange earthly wisdom for heavenly wisdom by taking up God's offer. The choice is ours.

Chapter Thirty-One

The Nature and Value of Wisdom

In this chapter we explore more about the nature and value of wisdom, that special gift which God gives to all who ask him for it. We start with something that Paul wrote to the Ephesians, where he says that he keeps asking God to give them the Spirit of wisdom and revelation (Eph. 1:17). Paul sees this as urgent and essential. In particular, he keeps asking as he knows that such wisdom is not a one-off gift, delivered in its entirety in one batch, but something that is needed on a regular basis.

Also in this prayer for the believers in Ephesus, Paul links wisdom with revelation. He mentions revelation not as something separate from wisdom but as an integral part of it. He wants to stress that wisdom is not about the accumulation of facts or the application of reason, nor is it merely gaining more information or knowledge. Rather, wisdom reveals things to you that you wouldn't otherwise know.

It is important to realise that being wise is not about knowing lots of things, being smart or becoming learned. It is not based on intelligence or reliant upon a high IQ, nor is it exclusive to those considered to be clever. In fact, clever people are not always the wisest. You may have noticed this! In reality, cleverness can get in the way of wisdom, blocking out the sense of any need for wisdom from God. It may create earthly wisdom, but as we have seen before from James 3:14, this merely promotes envy, selfish ambition, boasting and the denial of truth.

Of course, there is nothing wrong with education generally or with learning new things. As I shared before, my ambition in early life was to (eventually!) become a wise old man, but as a young man I still went to university. I studied mathematics and then taught it to others. But this did not in itself make me any wiser. Education is good, learning is fine. Get as much as you can, but also realise that this is not the same as wisdom.

My education helped me get a job and earn a living, but earning a living is not the same as living a life. The world often confuses these. It urges you to earn more money and acquire as many material things as possible. But God's wisdom is not measured in such ways. Rather it is about how to live a life successfully; not so much about your *standard* of living but your *standards* in life. In short, knowledge may increase your income, but wisdom improves your outcome.

Wisdom may draw upon our existing knowledge and skills, but it goes beyond them, and takes us further. Wisdom helps us apply what we already know and can do, especially in situations that would otherwise defeat us. Its benefits are many. Wisdom helps us survive in difficult circumstances, and avoid tricks and traps that might otherwise destroy us. It alerts us to deception, fake news, lies and half-truths. It protects us and guards our life when danger threatens. It indicates the right direction to follow and the correct path to take. Above all, being wise is about making better decisions and good choices.

By way of illustration consider the humble tomato. Knowledge tells you it is a fruit; wisdom tells you not to put it in a fruit salad. This light-hearted quip, originally attributed to Miles Kington, humourist and journalist, is now legendary, almost proverbial in its own right. For instance, its use by Brian O'Driscoll, Ireland's Rugby captain, ahead of their Six Nations clash with England in 2009, is an amusing example of how it attained fame. Do Google this!

As well as raising a smile, this tomato-based witticism expertly expresses the difference between knowledge and wisdom. It also stresses that wisdom is essentially practical – and not just for improving the taste of your meals! It equips you for whatever task God gives you, whether relatively mundane or a large-scale spiritual venture.

Wisdom enables you to get things right that you wouldn't normally get right if you relied solely on your own skills or knowledge. It provides something extra, and puts to better use what you already know or can do. In summary, wisdom is knowing what to do when you don't know what to do, knowing what to say when you don't know what to say, knowing where to go when you don't know where to go.

For instance, in the gospels Jesus warned his disciples they would one day be brought before synagogues, rulers and authorities, but they were not to worry about how to defend themselves or what to say at these difficult times. Jesus assured them, 'I will give you words and wisdom that none of your adversaries will be able to resist or contradict' (Luke 21:15). This is repeated elsewhere with a slight variation that it would be the Holy Spirit who would teach them what to say at such times (Luke 12:11-12, Matt. 10:18-20). This variant form amounts to the same thing. God-given wisdom to the rescue!

As well as knowing what to say and when to say it, part of being wise is realising that it might be better not to say anything at all. One of the Old Testament wisdom books asserts that there is 'a time to be silent and a time to speak' (Eccles. 3:7b). This is part of a longer passage which says there is a right time for everything and also for its opposite (Eccles. 3:1-8). Wisdom helps us decide which course of action is the correct one and when to take it. Sometimes the same set of circumstances may require a different approach at different times. Here is another aspect of life which requires a wisdom often beyond our applicable skills or usual understanding of such matters.

We have repeatedly stated that wisdom is about making better decisions and one aspect of this is knowing the right time to make a decision. This can be crucial. Making a decision straightaway, or too early, may be disastrous. In such cases the correct decision is to *not* make a decision, or at least to delay it. We need to resist the temptation to rush into a decision too soon. But on the other hand, indecision could also be harmful. So what do we do? Do we 'look before we leap' or is it a case of 'he who hesitates is lost'? Both are wise; both are true; but when do we trust one ahead of the other?

Overall, God's gift of wisdom provides an understanding of life and how it works, because it comes from the one who made us and gave us life. His wisdom will tell you personally how to get the most out of the particular life you have been given, how to successfully play the hand you have been dealt. As part of this, wisdom helps us in the more difficult times in our lives, times of suffering and disaster. It enables us to think through what has happened and possibly why. It counteracts knee-jerk reactions and negative responses which may not be helpful, such as getting angry with God or indulging in self-pity. Instead, wisdom can give us a correct perspective which then empowers us to make positive responses, such as compassion or patience. Wisdom often comes to the fore in such hard times.

Knowing God means reading his Word. Paul commends Timothy that from infancy he has known the Holy Scriptures, 'which are able to make you wise for salvation' (2 Tim. 3:15). Make you wise, notice, not clever, and in particular wise regarding salvation which is what really matters. Of course, by scriptures Paul meant the Old Testament, including the Wisdom books which we have been studying.

Finally in this chapter we consider something else from Paul. In 1 Corinthians chapter 12, Paul starts by saying he does not want us to be ignorant regarding spiritual gifts, one of which is a 'word' or 'message of wisdom' (v8). This is something spoken, perhaps given by God to you to speak to others. Here you may find yourself saying something you didn't expect or know about in advance but which provides wisdom to build up other believers or help an individual solve a problem in their life, unblock a situation, or put their life back on track.

So wisdom is a priceless gift but we note that it is not in itself a specific ministry. Wisdom is not included in any list of ministries, such as in 1 Corinthians 12:28 or Ephesians 4:11. There is no separate ministry of wisdom. Rather wisdom is given to underpin all other gifts and ministries. We all need it whatever our gift or ministry because, as we often see, any of these can be exercised unwisely.

Chapter Thirty-Two

In Conclusion

As we come to the end of our exploration of biblical wisdom, we ask whether what we have been learning still matters today. Has biblical wisdom anything to say to the average man and woman living in the modern world? Or is it too conditioned by its historical and religious context to be of any positive value now?

Some may claim that today's issues are very different from before, both in magnitude and complexity. Society has changed radically and so needs new wisdom to help it cope. It is commonly asserted that we must look to ourselves, rather than to the past, for any solutions to our needs. It is noticeable that such arguments about detaching ourselves from the past often reflect a desire to assert our independence from Almighty God or to justify a lack of belief in him.

However, in the final analysis our main concerns about life and death, justice and power, haven't changed that much. We still struggle to make sense of life and the overall human condition. We remain puzzled about a world where wickedness can thrive and even dominate, and where the innocent suffer. So is it really sensible to ignore the accumulated wisdom on these matters gained over the course of human history?

The biblical wisdom literature still has much to offer a world which for many seems constantly trapped in meaninglessness. It provides both a firm ground for believers and also a suitable meeting point for debate between Christians and others. We all live in the same world with similar life experiences, so we can reasonably expect that what biblical wisdom offers will interest all people. It can be a struggle to get a hearing for the Christian faith in our modern world but here is a chance to build bridges and engage in relevant discussions.

It is within such discussions that the diversity of the biblical wisdom literature is an asset. For some, Proverbs may display a rather rigid approach to right and wrong. Its assertion, or at least assumption, that righteousness is automatically rewarded and sin punished, may be not be entirely wrong but at times can seem a too simplistic outworking of cause and effect. But even if so, this is balanced out elsewhere in the wisdom literature. Other parts express doubt in these mainstream views or even question their validity. Ecclesiastes and Job fill out the picture by challenging this assertion and debating what happens when exceptional circumstances and crises occur.

The search for wisdom is as old as humanity itself, so the antiquity of biblical wisdom should be no barrier to today's inquirer. The wise man of any era is someone who seeks to understand his world, one into which wrongdoing has intruded and disrupted the perfect order.

Moreover, the idea that every human being must find the right path through life remains a realistic one. At birth everyone embarks on a journey. Where will it end? There are always alternative paths to choose between. Wisdom provides the road map so that the wise can journey with confidence while the foolish may easily lose their way.

While the ancient nature of biblical wisdom may not in itself be a negative factor, the objection may remain that it is still too tied in with Judaism, or the Judeo-Christian viewpoint in general, to be worthwhile today. However, although the biblical wisdom books may have an historical setting, they are not primarily based upon Israel's religious history or contextualised within their covenants or the Law.

Certainly the Jews canonised their wisdom literature as an expression of their life with God, but they did so from a creation perspective, a belief there is a fundamental order to the world and how it was created, an order that is discernible by experience to all. They also believed that the purpose of wisdom is to bring conformity to that order, but this is not the same as Law in the strict sense. If there is a relationship between wisdom and Law, it is an indirect one. They may share the same moral stance as both come from the same God and relate to his character, but whereas laws command, wisdom advises, warns and persuades.

Overall, the wisdom books are a significant part of the Old Testament canon. They hold their place alongside Torah and the prophets. But they also point ahead towards a greater wisdom to come in Christ.

Without Christ and the wisdom of God, all we have is self-help or human religion. If you haven't yet received Christ and his wisdom, then ask today. If you already know Christ, then go on asking for wisdom. It seems there is no limit.

A journey into greater wisdom awaits you. But we need to be continually receptive in order for wisdom to grow in us. It doesn't come all at once. Gaining more wisdom is part of Christian growth and discipleship, which needs time. So make sure to leave space in your life to seek God and pray for wisdom.

In this book we have been exploring biblical wisdom and listening to words from the wise. Let's end with some more of these:

> 'For the LORD gives wisdom; from his mouth come knowledge and understanding.' (Prov. 2:6)

Index of Scripture

Genesis

Gen. 3:6	264
Gen. 18:27	165
Gen. 22:12	34
Gen. 25:13-18	106
Gen. 25:14	106
Gen. 41:8	22
Gen. 41:16	22, 219
Gen. 41:33	22
Gen. 41:38-39	219
Gen. 41:39	22, 219

Exodus

Exod. 2:1-11	67
Exod. 3:6	33
Exod. 7:11	22
Exod. 14:31	32
Exod. 20:17	265
Exod. 20:20-21	32, 33
Exod. 22:26	92
Exod. 28:3	24
Exod. 31:2-11	24
Exod. 33:11	34
Exod. 35:30ff	24

Leviticus

Lev. 25:25	92

Numbers

Num. 24:3	107
Num. 24:15	107

Deuteronomy

Deut. 5:21	265
Deut. 5:29	33, 220
Deut. 6:1-2	39
Deut. 6:2	220
Deut. 6:20	39
Deut. 6:24	220
Deut. 7:1-2	242
Deut. 7:3	242
Deut. 10:12	33
Deut. 10:20-21	32
Deut. 17:14-20	241

Deut. 19:14	92	1 Kgs 10:2	240
Deut. 20:5	84	1 Kgs 10:3	240
Deut. 24:10-13	92	1 Kgs 10:14-25	241
		1 Kgs 10:5	240
1 Samuel		1 Kgs 10:6-7	240
1 Sam. 1	115	1 Kgs 10:8	240
1 Sam. 8:11-18	238	1 Kgs 10:13	240
		1 Kgs 10:14-25	241
2 Samuel		1 Kgs 11:1	244
2 Sam. 12:24-25	237	1 Kgs 11:1-4	242
2 Sam. 23:1	107	1 Kgs 11:4	244
		1 Kgs 11:6	244
1 Kings		1 Kgs 11:7-8	242
1 Kgs 2:2-4	244	1 Kgs 12:4	238
1 Kgs 2:19	114	1 Kgs 15:13	114
1 Kgs 3	238		
1 Kgs 3:3	244	**1 Chronicles**	
1 Kgs 3:5-15	230	1 Chr. 2	243
1 Kgs 3:16-28	239	1 Chr. 21:1	135
1 Kgs 3:28	239	1 Chr. 22	243
1 Kgs 4	241	1 Chr. 22:15-16	25
1 Kgs 4:29-31	68, 177		
1 Kgs 4:29-34	239	**2 Chronicles**	
1 Kgs 4:32	63	2 Chr. 6:2	243
1 Kgs 5:13-18	238	2 Chr. 6:18	243
1 Kgs 6:1	243	2 Chr. 6:33	243
1 Kgs 6:37	243	2 Chr. 6:34	243
1 Kgs 7:1	243	2 Chr. 6:38	243
1 Kgs 8:63	84	2 Chr. 7:5	84
1 Kgs 9	243	2 Chr. 20:7	34
1 Kgs 9:10-13	243	2 Chr. 29	243
1 Kgs 10	239		

Job

Job 1:1	33, 152
Job 1:3	133
Job 1:9	140
Job 1:14	133
Job 1:15-17	129
Job 2:9	136
Job 2:11	137, 164
Job 3:1	136
Job 3:1-42:6	127
Job 3	128, 141
Job 4:12-21	137
Job 5:2	212
Job 5:13	171
Job 5:17	142
Job 5:18-26	142
Job 5:19	111
Job 5:27	142
Job 7:13	165
Job 7:21	133
Job 8:8-10	138
Job 9:15	133
Job 10:15	133
Job 11:6	138
Job 11:7	138
Job 13:26	133
Job 14:16-17	133
Job 16:2	165
Job 18:5ff	212
Job 19	159
Job 19:25-26	173
Job 20	154
Job 21:34	165
Job 22	128
Job 23-24	128
Job 26	144, 145, 150
Job 26:2-4	145
Job 26:5-14	144
Job 27	144, 145, 150, 159
Job 27:1	150
Job 27:13-23	144
Job 28	52, 128, 148, 149, 150, 151, 153
Job 28:1-11	153
Job 28:12	9, 153
Job 28:13-20	153
Job 28:21-28	153
Job 28:23	153
Job 28:27	153
Job 28:28	29, 152, 154
Job 29:1	150
Job 29:7	133
Job 29:35	165
Job 30:19	165
Job 31:35	146, 147
Job 31:38-40	133
Job 31:40	146
Job 32:2-5	138
Job 32:8	133
Job 32:18	133
Job 33:4	133
Job 33:33	138
Job 34:1	150
Job 35:1	150

Job 36.1	150	Job 42:11	165
Job 36:27–37:13	147, 157	Job 42:16	130
Job 37:14	147		
Job 38:1	147, 157	**Psalms**	
Job 38:1–40:2	158	Ps. 1	221
Job 38:3	160	Ps. 8:4	110
Job 38:5	110	Ps. 9	117
Job 38:7	133	Ps. 10	117
Job 38:8	110	Ps. 14:1	43
Job 38:25	110	Ps. 25	117
Job 38:36-37	110	Ps. 34	117
Job 39:5	110	Ps. 32:8	266
Job 40:2	158	Ps. 37	94, 117
Job 40:3-5	158	Ps. 37:1-2	94
Job 40:4-5	159	Ps. 49	222
Job 40:5	160, 164	Ps. 49:1-4	223
Job 40:6–41:34	158	Ps. 49:15	223
Job 40:7	160	Ps. 73	223
Job 40:15	162	Ps. 73:4-5	223
Job 40:15-24	161	Ps. 73:6-11	224
Job 41:1-34	161	Ps. 73:13	224
Job 41:1	171	Ps. 73:15	226
Job 41:14-17	161	Ps. 73:16	224
Job 41:19-21	161	Ps. 73:17	225
Job 41:33-34	162	Ps. 73:18	225
Job 42:1-6	128	Ps. 73:18-19	226
Job 42:3	163	Ps. 73:21-22	226
Job 42:5	33	Ps. 73:23-24	226
Job 42:6	165	Ps. 73:26	226
Job 42:7	163, 171	Ps. 78	222
Job 42:7-9	155	Ps. 78:1	222
Job 42:7-17	127		

Index of Scripture

Ps. 78:1-3	222
Ps. 104:26	162
Ps. 107:25-27	95
Ps. 107:27	25
Ps. 109:6	135
Ps. 111	117, 221
Ps. 111:10	29, 221
Ps. 112	117, 221
Ps. 119	117, 222
Ps. 145	117

Proverbs

Prov. 1:1	38, 62
Prov. 1:1-7	37
Prov. 1:2	41
Prov. 1:4	42
Prov. 1:5	42
Prov. 1:7	29, 42, 119
Prov. 1:8	39, 72, 114
Prov. 1:8-9	37
Prov. 1:9	72
Prov. 1:10-19	39
Prov. 1:17	39
Prov. 1:20-33	46
Prov. 1:29	29
Prov. 2:5	29
Prov. 2:6	278
Prov. 3:1-4	41
Prov. 3:7	29
Prov. 3:11	72
Prov. 3:12	72
Prov. 3:13-18	46
Prov. 3:19-20	49
Prov. 3:34	104, 255
Prov. 4:6-9	46
Prov. 4:11-19	248
Prov. 4:18-19	45
Prov. 5:3-8	46
Prov. 6:1	92
Prov. 6:6-11	97
Prov. 6:10-11	97
Prov. 6:16-19	111
Prov. 6:20	114
Prov. 6:20-35	39
Prov. 6:27-28	39
Prov. 7:24	39
Prov. 7:4	46
Prov. 8	46, 51, 53, 61, 122, 232
Prov. 8:4-11	48
Prov. 8:12	55
Prov. 8:12-14	48
Prov. 8:13	29, 48
Prov. 8:15-21	48
Prov. 8:22	49
Prov. 8:22-30	55
Prov. 8:22-31	48
Prov. 8:23-26	49
Prov. 8:24	49
Prov. 8:25	49
Prov. 8:27-29	49
Prov. 8:30	49, 50
Prov. 8:30-31	50
Prov. 8:32	51
Prov. 8:35	58

Prov. 9	21, 37, 45, 46, 47, 51, 52, 53, 54, 59, 61	Prov. 19:23	29, 32
		Prov. 22:4	29
		Prov. 22:6	77, 79, 82, 83, 84, 85
Prov. 9:4	56		
Prov. 9:5	57	Prov. 22:17	9, 20, 62, 65, 90, 105, 114
Prov. 9:6	57, 58		
Prov. 9:10	29	Prov. 22:17-21	89
Prov. 9:13	57	Prov. 22:17–24:22	65
Prov. 9:14	55	Prov. 22:17–24:34	62
Prov. 9:13-15	56	Prov. 22:18	90
Prov. 9:16	56	Prov. 22:19	91
Prov. 9:17	56, 57	Prov. 22:22-23	91
Prov. 9:18	55, 57	Prov. 22:24-25	91
Prov. 10	60, 61	Prov. 22:26-27	92
Prov. 10:1	38, 62, 71	Prov. 22:28	92
Prov. 10:1–22:16	61, 62	Prov. 23:1-3	92, 93
Prov. 10:5	80	Prov. 23:4-5	93
Prov. 10:6	80	Prov. 23:6-8	93
Prov. 10:12	104	Prov. 23:10-11	92
Prov. 10:27	29	Prov. 23:11	90, 92
Prov. 11:1	71	Prov. 23:12	90, 94
Prov. 11:15	92	Prov. 23:13-14	94
Prov. 12:1	80	Prov. 23:17	29
Prov. 12:4	118	Prov. 23:17-18	94
Prov. 14:26-27	29, 32	Prov. 23:17–24:22	89
Prov. 15:1	71	Prov. 23:29-35	94
Prov. 15:16	29	Prov. 23:30	95
Prov. 15:33	29	Prov. 23:32	95
Prov. 16:6	29	Prov. 23:34	95
Prov. 16:10-15	63	Prov. 24:10	96
Prov. 16:31	71	Prov. 24:11	96
Prov. 17:18	92	Prov. 24:19-20	94
Prov. 17:19	81	Prov. 24:21-22	96

Prov. 24:23	97	Prov. 30:17	111
Prov. 24:30-34	97	Prov. 30:18	111
Prov. 25–29	62, 97, 99, 101	Prov. 30:20	111
		Prov. 30:21	111
Prov. 25:1	62, 64, 100	Prov. 30:24-28	25
Prov. 25:2	102	Prov. 30:29	111
Prov. 25:2-7	63	Prov. 30:33	112
Prov. 25:3	81	Prov. 31:1	106, 113
Prov. 25:25	82	Prov. 31:1-9	114, 117
Prov. 25:6-7	102	Prov. 31:2	115
Prov. 25:11	72	Prov. 31:3	116
Prov. 25:21-22	103	Prov. 31:6-7	116
Prov. 26:4-5	76	Prov. 31:10-31	63, 116, 117
Prov. 26:9	76		
Prov. 26:11	102	Prov. 31:10	117, 118
Prov. 26:14	72	Prov. 31:15	118
Prov. 27:1	102	Prov. 31:20	118
Prov. 27:15	72	Prov. 31:22	118
Prov. 27:17	102	Prov. 31:23	118
Prov. 28:14	71	Prov. 31:26	119
Prov. 30	62, 104, 105, 220	Prov. 31:28-31	119
Prov. 30:1	105, 106, 107, 108	Prov. 31:30	119

Ecclesiastes

Prov. 30:1-3	109	Eccles 1:1	176, 179, 180, 182
Prov. 30:1-4	109		
Prov. 30:2-3	109	Eccles. 1:2	180, 182, 186, 200
Prov. 30:4	110		
Prov. 30:5	109, 110		
Prov. 30:5-6	109	Eccles. 1:2-11	182
Prov. 30:7	109, 111	Eccles. 1:3-11	190
Prov. 30:11	111	Eccles. 1:3	187
Prov. 30:15	111		

Eccles. 1:9	190
Eccles. 1:12	176, 180
Eccles. 1:12–6:9	182
Eccles. 1:13	188
Eccles. 1:14	187
Eccles. 1:16	176
Eccles. 2:11	187
Eccles. 2:17	187
Eccles. 2:26	187
Eccles. 3:1-8	190, 272
Eccles. 3:7b	76, 272
Eccles. 3:11	191
Eccles. 3:19-21	192
Eccles. 4:2	193
Eccles. 4:2-3	197
Eccles. 4:3	193
Eccles. 4:4	187
Eccles. 4:16	187
Eccles. 5:18–6:2	194
Eccles. 6:9	187
Eccles. 6:10-12	182
Eccles. 6:10–11:6	182
Eccles. 6:12	195
Eccles. 7:1	194
Eccles. 7:1a	195
Eccles. 7:2	194
Eccles. 7:11-12	195
Eccles. 7:13-14	195
Eccles. 7:19	195
Eccles. 7:23-24	195
Eccles. 7:25	188
Eccles. 7:26	196
Eccles. 7:27	180, 181
Eccles. 7:28	196
Eccles. 7:29	196
Eccles. 8:11	197
Eccles. 9:1-10	197
Eccles. 9:4	197
Eccles. 9:10	198
Eccles. 9:11	198
Eccles. 10:1	198
Eccles. 10:20	198
Eccles. 11:1	198
Eccles. 11:2	198
Eccles. 11:7	198
Eccles. 11:7–12:8	182
Eccles. 12:1-7	198, 199
Eccles. 12:6-7	199
Eccles. 12:8	180, 182, 200
Eccles. 12:9	40, 178, 180, 183, 193
Eccles. 12:9-10	212
Eccles. 12:9-11	181, 205
Eccles. 12:9-14	182, 200
Eccles. 12:10	180
Eccles. 12:12	200
Eccles. 12:13	182, 215

Isaiah

Isa. 11:2	248
Isa. 27:1	162
Isa. 29:14	251
Isa. 33:6	31
Isa. 40:12-14	110
Isa. 40:20	25

Isa. 41:8	34		Amos 2:4	220
Isa. 43:1	31		Amos 2:6	220
Isa. 43:5	31		Amos 3:3-6	220
Isa. 44:2	31		**Obadiah**	
Jeremiah			Obad. 8	23
Jer. 10:9	25			
Jer. 18:18	40		**Zechariah**	
Jer. 23:4	107		Zech. 3:1-2	135
Jer. 23:11	107			
Jer. 23:12	107		**Matthew**	
Jer. 25:20	129		Matt. 2:1-2	23
Jer. 50:35	23		Matt. 5:45	66
			Matt. 6:22-23	93
Lamentations			Matt. 7:7-8	258
Lam. 4:21	129		Matt. 7:13-14	59
			Matt. 7:13-27	248
Ezekiel			Matt. 7:24-27	59
Ezek. 27:8-9	23		Matt. 10:18-20	272
			Matt. 12:42	
Daniel				
Dan. 2	23		**Luke**	
Dan. 2:20-23	23, 220		Luke 2:52	248
Dan. 2:27	23, 220		Luke 11:31	207, 247
			Luke 11:40	248
Amos			Luke 12:5	35
Amos 1:3	220		Luke 12:11-12	272
Amos 1:6	220		Luke 13:18-19	69
Amos 1:9	220		Luke 14:7-11	102
Amos 1:11	220		Luke 21:15	272
Amos 1:13	220		Luke 22:31	170
Amos 2:1	220		Luke 22:53	171

John
John 2:19	86

Acts
Acts 2:43	35
Acts 5:11	35
Acts 7:22	67

Romans
Rom. 6:23	256
Rom. 8:15	35
Rom. 8:19-23	208
Rom. 11:33	254
Rom. 11:35	171
Rom. 12:20	103
Rom. 15:4	222

1 Corinthians
1 Cor. 1:24	18, 207, 247, 249
1 Cor. 1:18-25	251
1 Cor. 1:30	250
1 Cor. 2:1	252
1 Cor. 2:6-7	252
1 Cor. 3:19	171
1 Cor. 10:1-11	222
1 Cor. 10:13	171
1 Cor. 12:8	273
1 Cor. 12:28	274

2 Corinthians
2 Cor. 5:11	35

Ephesians
Eph. 1:17	269
Eph. 4:11	274

Colossians
Col. 2:2-3	250

2 Timothy
2 Tim. 3:15	273, 267
2 Tim. 3:16	203

Hebrews
Heb. 1:1	122
Heb. 11:24	67
Heb. 12:2	256

James
Jas 1:5	255, 256
Jas 1:5-8	256
Jas 1:6-8	257
Jas 1:17	258
Jas 2:23	34
Jas 3:13-15	263
Jas 3:13-18	23, 256
Jas 3:14	270
Jas 3:15-17	19
Jas 3:17	263
Jas 4:6	104, 255
Jas 4:13	256
Jas 4:13-17	102
Jas 5:1	256

Jas 5:11	125, 256	**2 Peter**	
Jas 5:20	104	2 Pet. 2:22	102
1 Peter		**1 John**	
1 Pet. 1:17	35	1 John 4:18	34
1 Pet. 4:8	104		
1 Pet. 5:5	104		

Wisdom of Ben Sirach

Wisdom of Ben Sirach 1:1–24:29	233
Wisdom of Ben Sirach 1:1-20	233
Wisdom of Ben Sirach 1:14	232
Wisdom of Ben Sirach 4:11-19	233
Wisdom of Ben Sirach 6:18-31	233
Wisdom of Ben Sirach 14:20–15:8	233
Wisdom of Ben Sirach 16:24–18:14	233
Wisdom of Ben Sirach 22:27–23:6	233
Wisdom of Ben Sirach 24	51
Wisdom of Ben Sirach 24:1-29	233
Wisdom of Ben Sirach 24:3	52
Wisdom of Ben Sirach 24:9	52
Wisdom of Ben Sirach 24:30–39:11	233
Wisdom of Ben Sirach 33:7-15	233
Wisdom of Ben Sirach 36:1-17	233
Wisdom of Ben Sirach 38:24–39:11	233
Wisdom of Ben Sirach 39:12–50:24	233
Wisdom of Ben Sirach 42:15–43:33	233
Wisdom of Ben Sirach 44–49	234
Wisdom of Ben Sirach 50	234
Wisdom of Ben Sirach 50:27	231

Wisdom of Ben Sirach 51:1-12	234
Wisdom of Ben Sirach 51:13-30	234

Wisdom of Solomon

Wisdom of Solomon 1–5	229
Wisdom of Solomon 6–9	229
Wisdom of Solomon 6:1	229
Wisdom of Solomon 7–8	52
Wisdom of Solomon 9	230
Wisdom of Solomon 10–19	229

The Instruction of Amenemope (or Amenemopet) — 65, 89, 90

Also available by Paul Luckraft

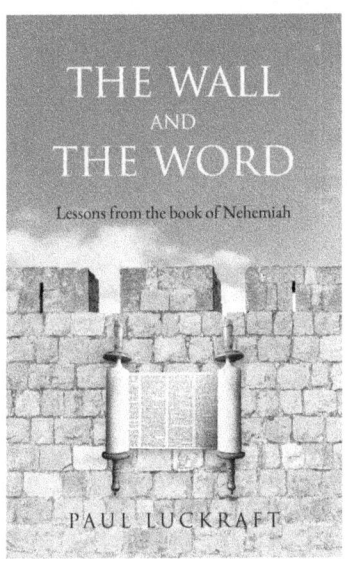

The Wall and the Word

ISBN: 978-1-915046-54-3

Nehemiah is best known for its account of the rebuilding of the wall of Jerusalem by the Israelites on returning from exile. But there is much more to the book than this. Equally important was the need to rebuild the people as God's community. How could they be reformed to live according to his will? For this they needed to rediscover what God had said in the Book of the Law.

Paul Luckraft examines each chapter to draw out the main lessons. Why did Nehemiah face a lot of opposition from many enemies, and what can we learn from his experiences? What exactly was this 'Book of the Law' and is this relevant to us now? Why was rediscovering the Feast of Tabernacles so important for them, and what can this mean for us?

Nehemiah is a largely forgotten book, but an essential part of our 'God-breathed' scripture. It's time to let it breathe again as we seek to rebuild ourselves as a community of believers and strengthen our own lives in his service.

Listening to the Jewis Jesus

ISBN: 978-1-915046-65-9

Nominated for CRT Christian Life Book of the Year 2024

Paul Luckraft's book explores the Hebraic nature of the teaching of Jesus and shows how a first-century rabbi spoke to other Jews of the time and in particular taught his disciples. What can we expect to find from such an exploration, and what can this mean for us today? Jesus used many Hebraic idioms, expressions commonly used in one language but which make less sense in another. Someone outside the culture or who is not a native speaker can easily be confused. A better grasp of such Hebraisms within the gospels will greatly improve our understanding of what Jesus is saying to us. In his teaching Jesus often hinted at the Jewish scriptures, employing the rabbinic technique of remez. These allusions to the Old Testament would be readily picked up by his listeners but we can miss them. We need to find these and unpack the depths of their meaning. Jesus' teaching also reflects aspects of first-century Judaism with which we are largely unfamiliar and need to appreciate more fully. One of these is the relationship between a rabbi and his disciples, a theme which occupies the first part of the book. This book will help those who teach the Bible as well as provide a companion for anyone wanting to read the gospels more accurately and follow Jesus more closely.

www.ingramcontent.com/pod-product-compliance
Lightning Source LLC
Chambersburg PA
CBHW060352110426
42743CB00036B/2751